New American Book of the Dead

IDHHB,

PUBLISH

1981

Editors: David Christie
Jerome Berman
E. J. Gold
Kay Waltzer
Josephine Fox
Typesetting: Nancy Christie
Wayne Hoyle
Tabatha Jones
Original Illustrations: Thomas Johnson
Cover Painting: Anna Flatten

ISBN: 0-89556-029-1
Library of Congress Catalog Number: 81-82579

Foreword

This new edition enhances the impact of this striking and exciting book. Here in short form is the substance of basic human esoteric teachings given in modern and current American (U.S.) consensus (below 40 year olds) language.

What is more important in one's here-and-now belief systems (simulations of Reality) than those clustering around one's Birth, Death, and apparent Re-Birth? Can we escape this repetitive round of incarnation-carnation-excarnation? Is there a Someone who can be free of this repeating tape-loop of Existences, of repeated Human-non-human states of Being? If there is, that Someone may need help to get off the round, the eternal dance in a circular path and enter other Domains beyond it. This book is one set of understandable injunctions on how to escape, or how to choose a more satisfying trip on the next choice-point: at Death, at Rebirth, during Transit.

Stimulated by this book plus the *Simulations of God,* I wrote and narrated an ECCO Training Film: *Simulations of God* (In Reality, of course, ECCO wrote it with me as their agent).

What is ECCO? In order to give one an understanding, I quote from chapter Zero of *Dyadic Cyclone* (written with my lady Antonietta).

"Several years ago, I enunciated a format (a principle) for such a concatenation of events, somewhat as follows:

"There exists a *Cosmic Coincidence Control Center* (CCCC), with a Galactic substation called *Galactic Coincidence Control* (GCC). Within GCC is a *Solar System Control Unit* (SSCU), within which is the *Earth Coincidence Control Office* (ECCO, sometimes mistakenly shortened to ECO, as in ECOSYSTEMS and in ECOLOGY — the study of Earth Coincidence Control Office). Down through the hierarchy of Coincidence Control (from Cosmic to Galactic to Solar System to Earth) is a chain of command with greater and greater specification of regulation of Coincidences appropriate to each level in the system. The assignments of responsibilities from the top to the bottom of this system of control is by a set of regulations, which, translated by ECCO for us human beings is somewhat as follows:

"To all humans:

If you wish to control coincidence in your own life on the planet Earth, we will cooperate and determine those coincidences for you under the following conditions:

1. You must know/assume/simulate our existence in ECCO.
2. You must be willing to accept our responsibility for control of your coincidences.
3. You must exert your *best capabilities* for your survival programs and your own development as an advancing/ advanced member of ECCO's earth-side corps of controlled coincidence workers. You are expected to use your best intelligence in this service.

4. You are expected to expect the unexpected every minute of every hour of every day and of every night.

5. You must be able to remain conscious/thinking/reasoning no matter what events we arrange to happen to you. Some of these events will seem cataclysmic/catastrophic/overwhelming: remember, *stay aware, no matter what happens/apparently-happens to you.*

6. You are in our training program for life: there is no escape from it: we (not you) control the long term coincidences. You (not we) control the shorter term coincidences by your own efforts.

7. Your major mission on Earth is to discover/create that which we do control: the long term coincidence patterns; you are being trained on Earth to do this job.

8. When your mission on planet Earth is completed, you will no longer be required to remain/return there.

9. Remember the motto passed to us (from GCC via SSCU): '*Cosmic Love is absolutely Ruthless and Highly Indifferent: it teaches its lessons whether you like/dislike them or not.*'"

(End of Instructions)

Now read this book, cover to cover. Watch out! It can be seductive. ECCO (through Gold) set up a beautiful trap for you. After you read it, ask yourself "What is the trap?"

If you can correctly answer that question, you are free.

— *John C. Lilly, M.D.*

New American Book of the Dead

Editor's Preface to the Sixth Edition

The *New American Book of the Dead,* in this fully revised edition, is the first complete version of a Book of the Dead available today. Unlike the *Tibetan Book of the Dead* which contains only two weeks of the seven week cycle for the Second Stage of Transit, the *New American Book of the Dead* contains the reconstruction of the entire seven weeks of the Intermediate State.

Buried for protection against religious fanaticism soon after it was written by Padma Sambhava, the *Tibetan Book of the Dead* was rediscovered hundreds of years later missing the last five weeks of the Second Stage of Transit. This is why week three through week seven seem so sketchy when compared with week one and week two, the weeks of the Friendly and Wrathful Deities. In the *New American Book of the Dead* which you hold in your hands, the entire seven week cycle of the Second Stage and the instructions for phenomenal rebirth are restored.

This particular edition of the Book of the Dead is not only a complete representation of the entire Transit cycle, but it is the first example of its kind in modern Western Judeo-Christian terminology and symbolism, in which Angelic Entities can be invoked as Guides for each of the forty-nine Chambers of the Second Stage of Transit.

Each week is a different Hall, or passageway through a definite series of Chambers which always appear in the same sequence. Each Hall is a unique vision of the non-phenomenal world. The incomplete visions of the Friendly and Wrathful Deities are now perceived through the veils of Thoughts and Emotions, to be followed, in descending order, by the veils of Apprehensions, Significances, Sensations, Manifestations and Reactions.

The old Tibetan system refers to each day within a week as a different world; in the *New American Book of the Dead,* these are called Chambers. They can also be defined as those qualities which cause ejection, or rebirth, from the non-phenomenal world of Transit into the phenomenal world. The series of Chambers can be described by the following adjectives: animal, saintly, chaotic, neurotic, human, possessive and brute. The entire process of Transit readings from the Clear Light of the non-phenomenal world to the Third Stage Rebirth readings trace a gradual downspiralling which ends in ejection from the non-phenomenal world.

Contents

Prologue

The New American Book of the Dead is a series of invocations. The book cover, type style, color and texture of paper, ink — all are part of the power of the Book. A book can be both the Mystery and the Key to the Mystery. When the pages are turned to a specific chamber, that chamber is invoked, even if it is not read. If the reader is angry, he can look in the Book to see what chamber he is in, then turn the page to enter another chamber and change his mood and manifestations. He can use the turning of the pages to be in any chamber he chooses.

One may downspiral, but by remembering the Four Lines:

All phenomena is illusion;
Neither attracted nor repelled;
Not making any sudden moves;
My habits will carry me through.

one can always return to
The Beginning.

Glimpses of Truth

I awaken from a dreamlike state and find myself in a musty, dimly lighted theater in which I have been watching the drama of reality. I look around and see my former selves filling the theater, absorbed in the drama on the empty screen. I try to get up and leave before I fall into sleep once again and the drama catches me in its fascinating grip.

As I walk out of the theater struggling against its magnetic attraction, I understand how I could have fallen into that trap again, becoming hypnotized by an unconnected set of emotional scenarios — how I could manufacture the sympathetic sensations that convinced me these things were happening to me as I fell into identification with the drama.

I realize with a sudden clarity of understanding that the events making up the time track are simply randomly connected emotional pictures associated by significance to each other, which only make sense *during* the dream. I have almost awakened from the dream, but real awakening is still before me. As I leave the theater a Guide offers to help.

"I didn't know they were part of it. It's a hard climb up. It feels as if we are at the top of a rollercoaster about to

let go. Can't we stop it? It's too late. Is there anything we can do to stop it? Do something. Get me home, quick. Hurry . . . I feel funny."

I become afraid, try to get away; I do not know what to do. All I want is to find some anchor point so I can orient myself, ground myself in some way. I want to hold on to something solid because my mind and identity are starting to disintegrate. If only I can find something firm on which to center, I can maintain.

My sensations are running wild; they no longer have a material form to control and buffer them. My sensations, perceptions and thoughts are starting to bother me. I feel as if I am at the top of a rollercoaster that is about to let go.

There is a rippling sensation of being torn apart at the seams. I can feel a yearning regret; an 'itchy' kind of feeling, as if I am exhausted far past my capacity, and yet it has hardly begun. I can see from here, the enormous effort I have been making to hold the ego together.

I am afraid to go insane, afraid I might already be insane . . . at the same time I know with a strange new clarity of understanding that I can never go insane or black out all the way to total unconsciousness, no matter how much I might wish to. I cannot forget.

My mind and logic center stop functioning. Except for my emotions and sensations I am alone. I no longer believe in the reality of the phenomenal world because I see behind it now; I know what makes it tick, but I do not know how to function without the intellectual functions of the mind. Yet I still have thoughts; I just can't seem to direct them.

The surroundings become unreal and flat. I am only able to relate to what is happening through feelings. Now it gives way to a feeling of high indifference about it all. I give up trying to fight to hold on to or direct it; I might just as well give up the struggle and let it happen.

"We're going too slowly. Everything just went flat. We're lost. Hurry . . . it's going to be too late."

The Guide has begun moving me toward the First Stage of Transit, which I have always called 'Home'. This is the safe space; once I get there I'm sure I will be all right . . . but we might not get there in time.

Everything and everyone in the surroundings is going flat again. Existence has taken on the quality of a dream, and I realize that 'I' am a figment of my own imagination. Everything that is happening to me happens according to an unchangeable script. Now I can see life as a mechanical machine without meaning or significance. There was never anyone there; none of it was real. All the parts were played by mechanical puppets.

I feel terror at the fakeness of it all; but we are going 'Home' — I'm sure that it will remain even when everything else dissolves. But what is taking so long? Could the Guide have become lost? We better hurry. It's happening faster now.

Finally we arrive. I have a weak urge to fight all this, but somehow I can't. If this space dissolves there won't be anything left I can depend on, so I allow it to run on. The drama is continuing, but now I can see this as just another dream.

"Hurry . . . I have to get inside. I can't breathe. I'm falling apart. I'm dying. Please help me. Why won't you help me?"

All the parts were played by mechanical puppets.

Fear is beginning to take me over as I try to fight off waking up still further. I am afraid of losing this little bit of ground that I have managed to hold. I still have an identity — I am either a human being who has become a little confused or one of three non-phenomenal entities who has been dreaming and has just awakened abruptly from a short nap.

Could the Guide have become lost?

"You know, don't you? It's still the same. It can't be true. Is this true?"
"Is what true?"
"This. This. This!"
"What's wrong?"
"You know what's wrong. Please help me.

"Are you real? I'm afraid. Oh, no, please turn it off. There are too many cycles within cycles. Where are we? Help me. Who is doing this? I can't go out there. I can't stay here.

"What's real?"
"What do you mean by real?"
"Please help me."
"Please help you what?"
"It's not true."
"What's not true?"
"You've got to help me."

"What do you want me to do?"
"Please help me."
"If you'll tell me what's wrong, maybe I can help you."
"I feel sick, I think I'm going to throw up."
"It might make you feel better."

I'm losing it — the more I try to resist it, the more I lose ground. Now I know exactly where I am and what's happening. I'm doomed to repeat this absurd drama forever. I don't have time to think.

"I think I'm dying. Please help me."
"What do you want me to do?"
"I'm dying. Oh no . . . ."
"What's wrong?"
"I can't die."
"You don't have to be into your body so much."
"I'm going to pass out.

"I have to lie down. I can't lie down. I'm so tired. Please help me. I need rest. I can't go on any more. It's going on and on. When do I get a chance to rest?

"I can't swallow or breathe. I can't hold on any longer. Help me. My teeth are chattering, they're so cold. I have to go inside. I can't stop."

I feel as if I'm dying. My breath is coming in gasps, and I feel weak and faint; I'm being revived only to go through it again and again. I feel as if I've been vomiting uncontrollably thousands of times. Finally it's over and I'm feeling incredibly weak and exhausted. All I want to do is lie down, but I can't.

The sensations are starting to happen again. The automatic actions of Transit are starting to take over; I'm losing control. I always used to feel as if I was in control.

Everything is going. I'm losing it . . . I wander helplessly and compulsively. I need time to think . . . That suddenly takes on a whole new significance as I realize that to think I have to have *time.*

"I can't die," I say, as if for the first time.

I've lost everything I was fighting to hold on to. It's all happening too fast. If only I could make it slow down I'm sure I could bring it back the way it was. I've come to the end of the line. Time has stopped flowing entirely. I'm afraid it's going to be like this forever. All I want to know is how to stop this from happening.

"I can't take any more. When does time start again? What time is it? Oh, no. Please help me."
"What's wrong?"
"When will it be over? The clock doesn't do anything."
"Of course not."
"There's a metallic taste in my mouth. My ears are clogged. Please help me . . . Hold me, I'm falling!"

I think of dying, but every time I've ever died I've ended up here, in the non-phenomenal world. I can't seem to die any more than this. The pain of the realization that I can't die saddens me . . . There is no escape. An intense feeling of regret builds up to a huge wave. With a shudder, I acknowledge it . . . "I can't die," I say, as if for the first time. Then I remember how many times I've said it before.

I seem to always be searching for something that will make it better, but it will never get any better. This is the way it is, always was, always will be. There isn't any time, so there isn't any change, in the non-phenomenal world.

In my wandering I want something to happen, but I don't know what. I'm looking for something . . . comfort, peace, rest . . . but I know I'll never be able to rest. Pacing restlessly from the 'kitchen' to the 'bedroom' to the 'bathroom' to the 'living room' . . . in the bathroom I decide to look at myself in the mirror. I feel a rising panic but I do it anyway. It's all right, it's still there.

"Your hair just turned gray. I feel old. Can't we slow it down? This is the end. How can you take this so calmly? I did that one already. This is it. It's never going to end."

I thought that being 'Home' was going to help, but I keep forgetting how I always feel when I'm here.
This will never end. I feel a rising panic; I don't want to be alone; on the other hand, I don't want to be with *them*.

"It's always the same room, always the same day. I've got to keep moving. I'm so tired. When do I get to rest? There's nothing out there. I'll just sit down for a while. I have to catch my breath. Something is going to have to change. I can't keep this up forever."

Irony without humor. The whole thing is absurd, but I only feel pain and fear. Why does it always have to be *my* trip? Finally I laugh, with a short, barking, coarse laughter. *"Of course,"* I say to myself as I surrender to it, *"this is how it is"*.

I don't want to always have to be the one. I wish there were someone else to take my place. I wish now more than anything else to be able to rest; to sleep and dream. Anything to have some peace from this terrible simplicity.

"Someone has to do it. Why am I always the one to have to do this? This is the part that I don't like. How long before I have to do that again? I'm sinking into the floor.

Why does it always have to be *my* ^{rrr}^r trip ^r ^r _{r?}

"How is it from there? It got brighter, didn't it? My face is sagging. The sound is getting higher. I feel all right, now. I'm really afraid, but I don't mind telling you about it. I know I'm acting ridiculous, but I can't help it. It's gone, now. It can never be the same again.

"This is a nice place we have here. It never changes, does it? When will it be over? I can't go to sleep until it's over. It's never going to end, is it? How much longer do we have to do this? Wow! I could never do this before."

I yearn for the solid predictable World . . . learning, exploring, developing; when there was still something unknown to find out about . . . when there were things I had to do, and I was getting somewhere . . . when it was all significant, and there were others just like me. How nice it was when I could depend on the walls to be solid and not breathe so disturbingly; when accumulating things meant safety, and if I didn't like it where I was, I could go somewhere else.

I would even settle for that now, knowing it isn't real, if only I could find some way of believing in and identifying with it.

"What a joke. Where have I been all this time? When is it my turn to go to sleep? Have you been here all this time? How long have you been doing this? Why is it always my trip? I'm always telling you my symptoms. Oh, I didn't know you did that one. Was that one you? What a joke that is. I feel very lonely."

I want something to prevent me from remembering this, but no matter how long I manage to sleep I keep coming back to this as if I never left it. I'm not sure what's real any more. "Real is anything I bump into," I remember. Wheels within wheels within wheels . . . all spinning inside each other in endless games within games. I don't know whether I have really awakened or it's just another dream.

Wheels within W heels within Wheels

"I'm probably shivering because it's cold. I can't stop shaking. It's getting bad again. I don't want to be the one to always do the talking. How much longer is this going to go on?"

I experience a few hundred lifetimes, but it's like the passing of a single breath. There is no relief here, and so I drift out of this realm into the next, searching for peace.

"Can't we do something else?"
"What would you like to do?"
"I don't know."
"You can do anything."
"I don't want to do this."
"What do you want to do?"
"I don't know. It's getting better."
"What did you do, just then?"

"I just became the wall. It seems like a million miles to my feet. My feet just disappeared. There are stars in my body. The earth is inside me, somewhere. Everything around here is a world. I don't want to make a wrong move. I can't move. I can't get down from here."

There is a sudden surge of power and certainty; the sensations have gotten better. Most of the pain is gone. We watch the drama go on, but we can't relate to it. We are fascinated with the idea of death and wonder what it would feel like. Playfully we decide some more beings to death so that we can observe their reactions.

I feel some entities rise up from the incarnations below, merging with my consciousness, aware of their struggle to maintain, as I did just a while ago. I am not concerned with them. They'll soon rise above all that incarnation and excarnation.

"There's no such thing as color. It's all done with mirrors. There's nothing out there at all. Is this all the space there is? It's all so simple!

"My arms are retracting. Where are we? I can't talk. Let's play charades. It sounds like . . . Ha Ha Ha Ha Ha. It got darker, didn't it? Which one is this? How about jumping or a side-step? I just disappeared. This body becomes anything it sees.

"I'm sinking again. Gravity is pulling me down. My legs are

There is no such thing as color. It's all done with mirrors.

melting down there. Too many sensations on this one. I'm the only one. Oh, one is a name. I'm one. I'm floating and in a stable state. I don't feel a thing any more. My hands just disappeared. I must have fainted. I have to have a body.

I'm sinking again. Gravity is pulling me down

"I don't think I'm ready for this. You tricked me. This is your fault. It was your idea; you suggested it. I thought you were the devil. We're always in space. The sun is a light bulb, isn't it?

"I don't want to touch anything alive. I would rather just watch this. The world is just a doll house. People are puppets. They're all just a pack of cards.

"There's a hole on the top of my head. No doubt about it, my skull just opened up. These legs feel like melting lead. It's getting bad again. How much longer, now? My face seems to be melting. I better get out of here and calm down. It seems to have stopped.

"I feel as if my stomach is going to explode. This can't go on forever. How do you turn this thing off? I just can't think. The skin is getting tighter."

Suddenly I find myself alone floating in blackness. With a shock I realize that I have been chosen once again as the sacrifice, and once again I understand: *there is no other to be the sacrifice.*

As I expand into the blackness I hope vaguely that something will happen to awaken me, but somehow I know that existence is just as much a part of my nature as non-existence.

It will go on and on, over and over; yet, since there is only one creation in one moment, it will all be the same. With a feeling of blissful ecstasy I resign myself; no one will ever come along from 'outside' to bail me out or help me escape, because there is no 'outside'. For ever and ever . . .

"I seem to have dozed off for a while. I don't understand a word you're saying. This body keeps dying on me. I'm tired of dying all the time.

WHAT HAPPENS NEXT ???

"All this has just been a dream.

"Why can't I go insane? How much longer does this go on? Can't we do something else now? What do you want from me?

"The pig eats toward the horse. Now I'm waiting here for the pig. When the pig eats me, I'll become the pig. I don't want to do this any more. Back and forth, back and forth. Can't we do something else?

My companion is calmly observing me, never cracking, remaining placid and undisturbed, not communicating, implacably and immovably *here*, managing somehow to stay calm through all this. I wish I could be so secure and solid.

"The light is pulsating. There's always a little chunk of space missing. Look in the corner, there. You can see that there's nothing out-

theeventsmakingupthetimetrackaresimplyrandoml yconnectedemotionalpicturesassociatedbysignifica ncetoeachother,whichonlymakesense*during*the dream.

"I wish I could go insane, then maybe I could get some rest. Time doesn't mean anything. You're doing this to me, aren't you? So this is how it all is. It just keeps happening over and over again. You've known about this all along. Everyone knew but me. You've been laughing at me all this time! What happens next?

"I'm not always this helpless. Usually I'm in control, but this is different. When is this going to end? You're going to destroy me, aren't you? I deserve it for everything I did wrong. It's getting better again. I was pretty paranoid there for a while."

side of here. What if this is all there is? I've been sitting in this chair forever. I've never left this room. It's all been a dream. Nothing matters. None of it is real. Why do I have to suffer? No one can help me. There's no one else. My ears are ringing. My head is buzzing.

"Something is happening. I'm starting to vibrate really a lot. A giant catapult is pulling back. It's getting ready to let me go. It's going to shoot me forward so fast I'll never be able to stop again. Everything is shaking! It's going to let go! No, not yet! I'm not ready for this! Slow it down.

"That's better. Everything looks lopsided. I can't stay here. How much longer is this going to go on? When will time be normal again? What time is it now? Did the hands on the clock move yet? It's always the same day, and it's always the same room. Is this as far as we can go? I'm going to have to lie down soon. How do you turn off the light?

"I just melted into the chair again. My back feels cold. The room just became the inside of my body. My face is inside this room. You're very old, aren't you? The floor just dropped away. It's millions of miles below me.

"It's getting darker. All worlds are inside my body. I can't move. I want to get out of here. I'm shaking again. My teeth are chattering. Why is this always such a big surprise? Why can't I remember when this is going to happen? I'm very, very cold.

the just became
ROOM
inside of my *WOOR*
body. *the*

"The more complicated it is, the safer I am. I feel safe, now. This is all there is to it. I set it up this way. Why didn't anyone tell me I was dead all this time? It's always the same. My body feels strange again. Another stage is coming on. I have to get out of here.

"This all seems very familiar, so ancient . . . This is the first time this is happening, again. Why am I following you around? I don't want to do this. I don't want to say stupid things. Why am I doing this?

"This room is alive. Wow! It really is alive. I'd like to apologize for the way I've been using you. If I'd known you were alive, I'd never have treated you the way I did. You're just waiting for a chance to have this body, aren't you? You're angry with me for being human, aren't you? I suppose I should give you a chance. I've really been a hog about it, haven't I? There's nowhere to run to, is there?

"I can't tell the difference. Isn't this the one I came in with? I just melted into you for a moment. I'm back now.

"Is this really happening? You suddenly look much bigger than me. That didn't last long. I keep coming back here. Every time I finally get into a body, it dies. There ought to be a better way than this. All those books say the same thing over and over again. I have to amuse myself for eternity. I did this to myself.

"I'll write up a future. The universe is a big joke on me. Why can't I black out all the way? I'll keep busy and keep moving. I'm beginning to forget. Now I'll kick in the mind. That seems to bring me down. Hide the key somewhere. Why is the key everywhere I look? I have to get control. Can't stop my thoughts . . ."

Why is the key everywhere I look? I have to get control.

INSTRUCTIONS
for the
READER

Reader and Voyager

Just as a midwife assists birth, the Reader assists the Voyager in the non-phenomenal world to achieve a good rebirth in the phenomenal world.

Instructions are delivered only through exact readings taken verbatim from the written text. Readings can either be given in the presence of the Voyager's body, through an article formerly possessed by the Voyager, or through a photograph of the Voyager's most recent phenomenal appearance, especially the face, taken as recently as possible.

If a photograph is used, it should be transported to the Reading Chamber in a light-proof container such as cardboard wrapped with aluminum foil.

The package containing the photograph should only be opened in the chamber in which the reading is to be performed. The purpose of using an article (photograph), sound (the name), or of reading in the presence of the organic body — is to establish a strong emotional bonding which will remain unaffected by disorientation in the non-phenomenal world.

The optimum method of establishing a solid bonding is to establish good communication and friendship before Expulsion. However, where there was little or no previous contact, it is possible to establish bonding by using the name, place of entry into the Transit State — such as a hospital, home or place of accident — age at time of Expulsion and a good physical description of the individual and, visualizing the form of the Voyager, reading to that visualized form.

While material objects may be used to make initial contact, the instructions are actually directed toward the Voyager in spiritual form. Definite sensations and perception changes are associated with bonding. Loss of contact can be tangibly felt by the Reader, usually indicating that the individual has taken rebirth.

If words in the readings seem blurry or unintelligible, one is probably not in contact, and the instruction may not be received. The Reader always understands the readings when contact is good and the bond has been established because *the clarity of the non-phenomenal world transfers by resonance from the Voyager to the Reader.*

If the Reader misses a word, the Voyager in Transit misses it, also. If that happens, one simply says: "I'll give that to you again."

Some of the sensations indicating that good contact has been established are:

1. *A tingling at the back of the neck.*
2. *A slight feeling of vertigo, as if the room tilted.*
3. *Hearing and visual perception greatly heightened.*
4. *An uncanny quiet during the readings, as if everything outside had suddenly come to a complete halt.*
5. *'A funny feeling in the gut' or 'the top of the head opened up'.*

6. 'Hearing things for miles and seeing through the walls'.

These and other signals tell us that we are in strong communication with the Voyager.

Our perceptions, sensations and feelings may be radically different from the examples given above, but one thing is certain — when we do definitely establish contact we get sensation and perception changes as we vibrate sympathetically.

This phenomenon is called *resonance*, the same phenomenon which occurs when we strike a tuning fork and hold it next to another similarly pitched tuning fork. The second tuning fork vibrates in resonance with the first even though the second tuning fork was not struck.

When we are *in resonance* with a

The power of the readings is in the *sound*, as well as in the meaning.

Voyager it seems to us as if we are reading to ourselves, but that we are someone else, liberated for the moment from our lower consciousness. We read aloud because the power of the readings is in the *sound*, as well as in the meaning.

Sounds can move a Voyager out of a difficult space in Transit and into another more usable space. Sound has the power to heal, liberate and awaken.

Making Expulsion an Important Event

We can help improve the chances for a good Transit Experience by arranging events surrounding *Expulsion* (the moment of separation and expansion out from the physical body) in order to help the Voyager release the bonds of attachment to his former incarnation before the shocks and disorientation of Transit.

The more we can make Expulsion an important event just as we do birthdays and weddings, the better the experience for the Voyager and the better for the family and friends, who will be much more able to allow the Voyager to be free to exit from the phenomenal world.

Under ordinary conditions a Voyager will go completely unconscious at the Expulsion stress-point and remain in a deep sleep-state throughout the Transit Experience unless he or she has prepared for Transit through definite exercises in much the same way one prepares for a sporting competition or any fast-breaking, stressful event.

Readings, even without preparation, can help the Voyager to remain awake and attentive to the events of Transit — even the most overwhelming situations.

When it is time to take rebirth, the Reader can help the Voyager choose an incarnation and perhaps avoid sudden, involuntary rebirth.

It can be said that the Readings partially make decisions of direction for the Voyager in Transit, because there is no mind with which to think, compare data, or make decisions. In Transit, everything seems to happen by reaction.

Of course this is not so vital for one who has learned *to make decisions with the Body of Habits*; however, even for those who have practiced the Teaching before Expulsion, it is a great relief for a Voyager to know that there will be readings of the Transit Instructions when they will be needed most.

Good non-phenomenal habits developed as part of our lifestyle help us to regard death and dying not as loathsome or fearsome, but as just another part of the space/time game. Organic rebirth in the phenomenal world is no longer a nightmare, just another dream.

The Job of the Reader

A doctor works to prevent organic death, but a Reader does not try to prevent natural death and dying. After all, this is the first real opportunity to get beyond the limitations of phenomenal world-hypnosis, in which we are blinded to the eternal world, since the previous voyage through Transit!

The post of Reader during the period of Transit is one of trust, dignity and integrity. Above all, a Reader must really care about the Voyager.

The readings are exact 'addresses' to the Voyager; they correspond *exactly* to each vital stress-point in the Transit sequence.

It is best to do readings at six in the morning and again at six in the evening. After a full week of such readings deliberately miss a reading. Notice that there is a definite feeling of unused energy. This special energy is why we do readings at the same time each day.

Constant practice and good reading discipline will develop a clear understanding of the function of a Reader for the Voyager in Transit. Good discipline will yield good results, but don't just sit there and think about it . . . Do it!

As we continue daily readings we are able to see other ways in which the Teaching can be applied: to prepare Voyagers while in the physical body; to examine deeper domains of consciousness; to balance the spirit to the organism in periods of retreat; as a spiritual healing technique; and many other applications not covered in the present volume.

Don't just sit there and think about it . . . *do it*

Transit Readings

It is especially important that the Reader be able to read aloud clearly and distinctly in order to provide vibrations strong enough that the Voyager in Transit will be sure to receive the instructions. Some simple but essential skills for reading are:

1. Read *slowly and distinctly*. Many readers sound at first as if they are trying to win a race. You will find that if you slow down even below the limit of slow speech tolerable for comfort, it will be just about right for delivering Transit Instructions.

2. Read the instructions *as if you had just thought of them*. Have them come from you. To really accomplish this, you should read the instructions at least a dozen times so you are familiar with them. Get a feeling of freshness about each idea as you read; feel the newness of each instruction as you encounter it.

3. Do not just *read* the book; *deliver the instructions*. 'Reading instructions' means that there is no one at the other end. 'Delivering instructions' means you can *feel* someone at the other end receiving and using them.

4. Read every instruction *as if it is urgent*. Get the idea of being an emergency radio operator giving instructions to a ship lost in a storm at sea.

5. Read *what is actually there*. If we sense the importance of these instructions for a Voyager in Transit, we will be careful to read the actual text and not something we substituted out of laziness. If we drift off we may give the wrong instructions or skip something important. *Give correct and complete data.*

deliver the instructions

These are some very simple techniques of communication which will make you more able to communicate to a Voyager in Transit. In fact, you will be more able to talk to friends, neighbors and co-workers if you follow these simple rules.

You should read the instructions at least a dozen
read the instructions
read the instructions
read the instructions
read the instructions
read the instructions
read the instructions
read the instructions
read the instructions
read the instructions
read the instructions
read the instructions

●
●
●
●
●
●
●
●
●
●
●
● ● ● ● ● ● ● ● **times**

Preparing
The Voyager

The optimal method of establishing good communication between Reader and Voyager is the establishment of good communication of Transit Instructions *before Expulsion*. If you are able to work with the Voyager while he or she is still physically present in the organic body, read as much of the book aloud as possible. Make sure you visit often.

If time permits, read the entire book through several times, and discuss what happens in each stage, allowing the Voyager to ask questions, meditate on the subject, and so forth. You might even read and handle questions so the Voyager knows what you are going to be doing during the time he or she is in the non-phenomenal world.

The section of this book called 'Instructions for the Voyager' is devoted to information about the Transit Experience and the exact sequence of events it contains. You should read as much as possible of this information to the Voyager before Expulsion, so that the Voyager is prepared for the events which will follow.

This section also contains exercises which can be used with the Voyager to prepare him or her to receive instructions from the Reader, and to better remain calm and centered throughout the unusual sensations of Transit. These exercises should be used as much as possible to establish and drill good Transit-habits before they are needed.

It is especially important to prepare the Voyager to recognize the sensations of Expulsion. The chapter *Sensations at Transition and Expulsion,* and the readings *The Symptoms* and *Transition* will give the Voyager the correct sequence of subjective impressions received during the phase of Ejection of Consciousness from the body, and the sequence of sensations resulting from the organism's shutdown process as these sensations are received through the nervous system and brain.

By knowing exactly what these sensations mean, the Voyager can smoothly enter and pass through the Expulsion point out of the phenomenal world and into the non-phenomenal, or eternal, world.

These sensations are similar to those received during illnesses such as flu, and through stress. When they occur during life but the body is not terminal, they cause pain and fear, triggering the death-expectation. When they occur at Expulsion, they are recognized as normal and natural sensations of a terminal condition. You can remove the pain and fear by removing the wonder and doubt — "Yes, you *are* terminal. Let's continue working with it."

Expulsion from the body always releases a great deal of energy, usually enough to allow the Voyager to remain in the Clear Light.

Remind the Voyager that a hospital is a place to go in order to get well, but that dying is not a sickness. If only people knew that birth and death weren't sicknesses, the culture would take a fast turn for the better.

If a Voyager decides to remain at home or to return home when it is known that he or she is definitely terminal, it will be much easier for you to open the way for contact during Transit, and also to prepare the patient better.

However, sometimes this cannot be arranged, and in any case, it is the Voyager's decision. You may decide to suggest this, but in each case the decision to give advice must be made in accordance with the patient's state, attitude and condition.

If the Voyager wishes to ask questions and discuss the readings, answer by referring to the appropriate passage in the book. You should be familiar with the book to the degree that you can quote chapter and section as the answer to a question about the Teaching. In this way you will be able to refer the dying person *directly to the source* for knowledge about Transit.

When you are reading to the Voyager before Expulsion, you should look at the Voyager with your mind's eye without having to look with your physical eyes. Direct your instructions and readings to the spiritual, non-phenomenal, part of the Voyager.

"Yes, you *are* terminal. Let's continue working with it."

Attending Transition

Transition is the period between the onset of the Symptoms of Expulsion from the body and the Vigil — the series of readings which take place in the hour following Expulsion from the organic form.

The time of Expulsion is drawing close . . . Make final arrangements for the readings: placement of a chair and table in the Transition chamber; the presence or absence of flowers and incense, as indicated by the Voyager previously if possible.

Make sure the family, friends and medical personnel expect you and won't make you wait for last minute confirmation of your mission.

Before you dash off madly to attend a bedside, make sure you know where the Voyager is going to be by the time you get there.

Before entering, say, "Blessings upon this house, and upon everyone in it, at the hour of passing."

Vigil:

If time allows, confirm arrangements for the delay in removal of remains during the Vigil. Make a definite point to do this and be sure to get the family's approval. It is a good idea to have someone else in the Transition chamber during the Vigil, and some states may have laws requiring two persons to be present.

If the family makes the point strongly enough, many hospitals, and certainly hospices, will allow Transition to be a family event — even a party — and not a lonely passage in a cold, clinical atmosphere.

If desired by the Voyager, a candle and incense can be placed on a side table and overhead electric lights turned off or dimmed. Soft, low lighting is best for easy passage and a mood conducive to contact with the Guide. The complete absence of electrical lighting is best.

If piped music comes into the Transition chamber over a loudspeaker system, either get it turned off or ask for the original soundtrack recording from *2001, A Space Odyssey*, or a soft, sweeping classical piece, like Sibelius' *Finlandia*, or *Concerto for Orchestra* by Bartok. Bloch's *Concerto Grosso* is also excellent as a mood setting for Transition. The Voyager may have and express some preferences in this area, also.

Now readings begin. If there is time, the Reader can review the entire book with the Voyager, but as soon as the first Symptoms of Transition appear, the readings for Symptoms should begin.

During the final moments before Expulsion and as much as two or three hours before, the Voyager will enter into a very calm, lucid and receptive state. At this point *the organic sensations will transfer to sensations of the non-phenomenal Body of Habits.*

Pain, if there has been an illness, may mysteriously vanish, leaving the Voyager with a feeling of 'lightening' as if floating upward. This is the authentic experience of what is called 'enlightenment'. This enlightenment and 'spiritual enlightenment' are exactly the same; they just take place at different times relative to Expulsion . . . Spiritual enlightenment is attempted much earlier.

In a hospital the medical staff sometimes insist that a body be removed or that all visitors including clergy leave the room. If this happens, don't panic; just ask for the chapel and begin readings there.

After the first hour it is all right to leave the room and for the body to be re-

the organic sensations will transfer to sensations of the Body of Habits, the non-phenomenal body

Now it is vital to establish good contact, because at this point the Voyager's consciousness is almost precisely divided between the two worlds.

Now the readings for the approach of Expulsion are begun. During the lucid period, the organic ego will deteriorate rapidly as a result of partial disintegration in the Clear Light. After this, Expulsion will be complete and the Voyager will move fully into the domain called *The Clear Light*.

Now the Vigil begins. When the Voyager passes fully into the Clear Light, the Reader begins to read the instructions for passage and for the domain of *Clear Light*.

Pain, if there has been an illness, may mysteriously vanish.

moved to a mortuary according to arrangements made by the family. Unless specifically invited to perform the services at the chapel, funeral home or graveside, the Reader's involvement with the family and friends of the Voyager is over unless they express a wish otherwise.

The Vigil is the most important part of passage because it establishes the contact and mood of the remainder of the Voyage.

It is at this vital period that the Voyager encounters the Primary, Secondary and Tertiary Clear Lights (Clear Light I, Clear Light II and Clear Light III). All Voyagers experience at least a moment or two, and up to several days, in the Clear Light.

Just as the organic ego learns by experience how to survive in the ordinary world, the Voyager in Transit must learn by experience to subdue the momentum of organic phenomena and be free from their effects and influence. Any pain or

discomfort felt by the Voyager now will be exclusively a result of suggestibility to phenomenal reverberations.

The Body of Habits is an exact duplicate of the organic body except that, while the organic body is controlled by thought and emotion in a socially organized process of conditioning, the Body of Habits is directed by a very primitive form of emotion called the *Emotional Body of Man.*

It can be said that the entire psychological makeup of human consciousness is emotional, since everything is 'filed' in the memory system by emotion and can be 'addressed' and found by searching in emotional patterns. The readings have very powerful effects on the Emotional Body, and this is what helps the Voyager keep steady in spite of disorientation and confusion.

During the Vigil, the instructions for the Clear Light are read continuously in repeating cycles for one hour (several Readers can read in shifts). All other subsequent readings are performed only twice daily — once at 6 A.M. and the same reading again at 6 P.M.

Preparation of the Body:

No post-mortem should be performed on the body under any circumstances whatever. Setting of features and cosmetics for open-casket service is all right, if performed at least sixteen hours following Expulsion.

A serious alteration of the body or removal of parts could compromise contact during the period of Transit, particularly the early period.

No embalming of any kind at any time. Refrigeration is fine. Burial is highly preferred over cremation.

The Voyager in Transit must learn by experience to subdue the momentum of organic phenomena and be free from their effects and influence.

Readings After Expulsion

The full cycle of Transit readings requires fifty-three days, as described in *The Transit Reading Cycle* below. Readings after Expulsion may be continued in the presence of the body until the burial or cremation, and it is sometimes valuable to do so in order to strengthen contact with the Voyager; however, at some point in the reading cycle, it will become necessary to continue the readings away from the body.

It may even be necessary to perform the Vigil Service away from the location of the body, if, because of the conditions of death, personal or family considerations of the Voyager, or practical considerations, the Reader is unable to be present at bedside at the time of Expulsion. In any of these cases, follow the *Recommended Procedure for Transit Readings* through the end of the reading cycle.

The Transit Reading Cycle

Day in Cycle	Reading
Day of Expulsion	Clear Light I
Day 2	Clear Light II
Day 3	Clear Light III
Day 4	Disintegration First Chamber
Day 5	Second Chamber
Day 6	Third Chamber
•	
•	
•	
Day 52	Forty-Ninth Chamber
Day 53	Third Stage Readings

All readings are read twice daily, generally at 6:00 A.M. and 6:00 P.M., or 7:00 A.M. and 7:00 P.M.

Recommended Procedure For Transit Readings

1. Decide what time each day you will do the readings. Transit readings are done twice a day, generally at 6 AM and 6 PM, although other times are often chosen in order to fit in with a Practitioner's other responsibilities. It is important to choose a time which fits easily into your daily schedule so you won't have to cancel or postpone readings.

2. Prepare your reading space. This space should be as separate as possible from the spaces used for other

functions, and should be clear of decorations, furniture, and any other objects which are not needed for the reading. Ideally, you should have a closed room set aside for this purpose. This space should then be thoroughly cleaned, vacuumed, mopped, walls washed, etc.

3. Set up the reading table. This should be a small table of convenient height for reading from a seated position. The table should be covered with a cloth, preferably pure white linen. Centered on this table should be a photograph stand.

Place a single votive candle in a clean *votive jar* in front of the photo stand. For the first and third stage readings, use a clear *votive jar;* for the second

stage readings, use a jar with the color of the cleansing radiation for the day of the reading.

Also on the table should be a small bell, an incense stand, flowers, offerings of water (in small cups), and optionally, a pair of taper candles to provide enough light to read by instead of artificial electrical light.

4. Once your reading table is set up, the area should be treated with respect. The only speaking in the reading space should be that of the readings, and you should allow yourself neither fidgeting nor sudden movements in that area. Upon entering and leaving the reading space, mentally reverberate the following prayer: "I wish this effort to be used for the benefit of all Beings everywhere."

5. Before beginning a reading, prepare yourself to enter the reading chamber. Leave all thoughts and associations of the phenomenal world behind, when you begin the reading.

6. Enter the reading space and make final preparations of the reading table. Light the candle and incense. The color of the votive jar (the color of one of the seven cleansing radiations) should be the same as the color given in the reading for the chamber of the Second Stage, and clear glass should be used for the First and Third Stages.

7. Unwrap the photo and place it on the photo stand. Ring the bell three times.

Behind **Leave all thoughts and associations of the phenomenal world , when you begin the reading.**

8. Open the reading in the following way: "This reading for the (title of reading) is addressed to the Voyager (name of Voyager)." Repeat the Voyager's name three times allowing it to resonate with the Voyager, making certain you have established good contact.

9. Begin the reading with, "I shall now begin the reading for the (title of reading)."

10. End the reading with, "This completes the reading for the (title of reading) directed to (Voyager's name). I shall read again for (Voyager's name) at (time of the next reading)." Ring the bell three times, extinguish the candle and seal up the photograph in its light-tight container.

11. After your reading is completed, leave the reading space quietly, again mentally reverberating the prayer, "I wish this effort to be used for the benefit of all Beings everywhere."

These instructions form a starting point for your readings. The more carefully and conscientiously you carry these out, the better your reading will be. Effective reading requires continual effort to concentrate your full attention and energies toward the goal of getting the instructions across to the Voyager in Transit.

"I wish this effort to be used for the benefit of all Beings everywhere."

Notes On Transit

"Hello — I've come to say, I cannot stay, I must be going . . . I'll stay the weekend through, I'll stay a week or two, but I am telling you . . . I must be going."

— *Groucho*

The experience of death ordinarily brings with it a period of forgetfulness and disintegration of the ego; we lose the connection of phenomenal events. Transit is the exact reversal of ordinary phenomenal consciousness.

Many cultures have been well-informed about preparing for the inevitable voyage through the non-phenomenal world at the end of the lifetime — but it is a matter of actually *doing* it — like going to the dentist.

In the Transit State, the Reader helps the Voyager to remain awake, alert and centered.

The Voyager may achieve complete liberation, or rebirth in a higher world. If rebirth in a lower world is inevitable, the Voyager can be guided into a good rebirth which may help him attain liberation.

This method has existed in every culture that ever appeared on the planet. There are as many books of the dead as there are variations of the teaching. There is a Tibetan book of the dead, a Coptic book of the dead, a medieval Western European book of the dead, a Mayan book of the dead, and an Egyptian book of the dead, *The Papyrus of Ani*, which uses drawings to indicate the progress of the Voyager through the Transit State. The Babylonian book of the dead is carved in the stone of architectural structures.

We do not even have words in the American language to describe the states between death and rebirth, although we do have words for the other three parts of Existence — 'Birth', 'Life' and 'Death'. One of the Four Parts of Reality is missing in the language — and the consciousness — of the Westerner.

Through the readings we can learn to bring into harmony and integration all Four Parts of Existence simultaneously.

The 'Invisible, Non-Phenomenal World' is only invisible because it is forgotten. To bring all parts of Reality into consciousness, and to be aware of the simultaneous existence of birth, life, death and Transit in every moment, is to increase our tolerance of eternity; to be able to see 'the Invisible King' who is our Endless Creator.

Hello—I've come to *SAY*, I cannot *STAY*, I must be going . . .

ITEM

The King's New Klothes: An Ancient Myth

Once — and only once — many years ago, so long ago even the passage of time had not yet begun, there was a King who was so fond of new clothes that He spent everything He had on them.

He had a different costume for every hour in the day, every day in the week, and every week in the year . . .

Nothing mattered to Him except His clothes; yet He was not satisfied with all the splendor of His wardrobe. Whenever His tailor came to Him, He continually asked for something new.

Eventually the tailor was driven to desperation; he could think of nothing new, and to make matters worse, he was the only tailor in the whole Kingdom.

So he thought and he thought, and eventually hatched a plan — a really diabolical idea. He told the King that he had invented a new fabric which not only changed colors and shape into a new costume every moment, but that it would reveal those who were dimwitted, ignorant or stupid, or all three by a wonderful property . . . to a fool the fabric would appear invisible, and to the wise, it would appear ever-changing and stunningly beautiful.

"What terrific clothes," the King thought to Himself . . . of course to Himself — always to Himself, "just by wearing them I will be able to distinguish the wise from the fools."

The tailor was commissioned to fashion the new clothes at once. Weeks went by, and still the clothes did not arrive; and no wonder, because there was nothing to send. The tailor never intended to make anything, because he had run out of ideas and, through cunning, intended to deliver nothing whatever to the King, after a suitable period of time had elapsed to convince the King that the clothes were incredibly difficult to manufacture.

Finally the new suit of clothes was delivered to the King, and He excitedly opened the package, only to discover that He could see nothing at all . . .

But, not wishing to appear dimwitted, ignorant or stupid or all three, He pretended to dress Himself in the new clothes and went out among the people in His Kingdom.

And do you think for a moment that any of His subjects risked their heads by mentioning anything about his nudity? Not on your life, they didn't!

Until a small child happened to say a little too loudly as the King passed by in procession, "Hey, look! The King is naked!"

A stunned silence passed through the crowd assembled there to witness the procession of the King and His ministers as the reverberations of the child's voice rippled across the square.

"just by wearing them I will be able to distinguish the wise from the fools."

"Now look at what you've done," the King wailed to the tailor. "Everyone thinks I'm a fool, going around naked."

"Nonsense, your Majesty," the tailor temporized. "Didn't they all see your ever-changing rainbow suit when you first emerged from the Palace? It's just the children who are unable to see it. Of course, they are ignorant. How could they know?

"I'll tell you what," he offered to the King, "I'll teach all the children to see your new clothes and, until they do, just ignore what they say about them."

The King thought this was a splendid plan, and the tailor was given the new job of teaching all the children to see His new clothes.

This went on for some time, but there was a flaw in the plan. In order to teach the children to see invisible — actually non-existent — clothes, and even to be-lieve it in spite of their senses, very strong methods had to be employed.

These methods of hypnosis were so powerful that, as the children became immersed in the hallucination of the King's clothes, their vision of the real world dimmed and, by the time they reached adulthood, although they could now see the King's new clothes, they were unable to see the King Himself.

When the King complained to the tailor about this, the tailor replied, "Well, what do you want more? Do you want them to be able to see you or your new clothes? You can't have both, you know."

The King was very aware that the necessities of conditioning were such that vision was extremely altered from the real to the hallucinatory. He did not have to be reminded that it was impossible to have subjects able to see both Himself and His new clothes. Of course, He could have returned to wearing His old clothes but, compared to an ever-changing infinitely varied rainbow-colored costume, even if it did happen to be non-existent, they didn't seem at all adequate.

"Hey, look! The King is naked!"

"How does this sound?" the tailor inquired. "I'll still teach all the children to see the clothes, but I'll teach a few of your subjects — not the wise majority of the population, because they are needed to support the Kingdom, but the fools, those who are useless to the general purposes of life in any case — to see you. Of course, you must realize that when they learn to see you and not your clothes, you'll appear to them to be naked . . . '' he added in a slightly apologetic tone.

"It's worth it," the King agreed. And so, some of the fools of the Kingdom — outsiders, misfits and those who, through some misfortune of nature were not content with hallucination — were taught to see the King.

And from that day to the present, the tailor has not been too awfully busy. And as for new ideas for new costumes for the King? Who needs aggravation?

The End

ITEM

Commentary on the myth of *The King's New Klothes,* or; Why Do You Say He's Naked? He's Not Wearing Any Clothes!

G. was approached by a group of his students who had been working intensively on the puzzling question of why most people see the King's clothes but they do not see the naked King Himself even though His clothes are invisible or non-existent as described in the children's fairy tale *The King's New Klothes.*

G. indicated there are clues from analogous situations in the phenomenal world, like sub-atomic particles. He pointed out that although we cannot see atoms we can see their effects so we know they exist. In the same way, although most people cannot see the King they see His clothes and some know that He exists.

"One of the things one must do in order to work is see the King, tear your gaze from the clothes. One must realize, and it is a big step to realize this, that either the King is naked or, if He is wearing invisible clothes, He *appears* to be naked.

"We know the King is naked, so what do we know of the Queen? She would be the clothes. If all phenomena is the King's clothes, why do we see just her, and not the King?"

T. replied, "She catches our eye."

"If she is invisible, *how does she catch our eye?*"

"We are invisible too," D. answered.

"And the King is not invisible," said G. "What keeps your attention, your vision, rooted to the phenomenal? Is there any way to see the King — to break through the veil of phenomena to see the King? Never mind why we would want to. Suffice it to say that in certain parts of work, it becomes necessary to see the King in all and everything.

"One cannot do this in ordinary ways, we can never come to it accidentally. The secret is safeguarded. Alone, one is unable to discover the exact method to see the King. Even with enough data, special help is necessary.

"The First Adam split into the Second Adam, plus Eve. Eve was tempted by Samael, who is also called Satan, in the Garden. How was a serpent able to seduce Eve?"

"Through sensing during the invocation of the Shekinah, who is the non-phenomenal part of Eve, and who remains in the Garden after the fall and expulsion from the Garden of the phenomenal part of Eve, you will discover that she is a serpent. You will know that the only one who sees Eve is Adam, her corresponding.

"Why, when Adam was seduced by his first wife, Lilith — a she-demon — were they not expelled from the Garden?

"Lilith was with the first Adam, Eve was with the Second Adam. Today, the children of Lilith are not serpents; Eve's children are serpents. If Eve was a serpent then all children of Eve were serpents."

"That is like the Jewish lineage," added J. "If the woman is Jewish, the children are Jewish. If the woman is a snake, the children are snakes."

G. continued, "If we are not snakes then we are not children of Eve."

"Who are we children of?" asked A.

"Lilith?" suggested L.

"That is one possibility, another is a demoness or fallen angel that cohabited with Adam . . . " said G. "Obviously we may have caught glimpses of the King, but we did not recognize the King. How would we recognize the King when we saw Him?

"In the Fourth Way we use a 'penetrating prayer' passed on from generation to generation, in the lineage of a school: Taking only what we know about the situation as a starting point, to penetrate any unknown, any mystery . . . "

"The only thing that is real is the King; everything we are involved with is illusion — the King's clothes," said J.

"The clothes are the only part of the King which appears to exist," added F.

G. said, "We do not see the King, we see His clothes, and that is all we see. But we know the King is naked; the clothes are invisible or non-existent. We are looking at something invisible or non-existent and seeing something. Because we are seeing the invisible or non-existent, we cannot see the King.

"It is not that nothing exists; the King is really there, it is only His clothes that do not exist. It is just the phenomenal world that is the illusion.

"How is it that we can be brought to such a condition that we can see His clothes, but not the King Himself? How is it that we have come to this condition where we can see the invisible and not see the visible? What does this tell us about our perceptions?"

"That we do not see what is there, we see a reflection," said T.

"We see upside down," said A.

"We are seeing hallucinations," added J.

"We are seeing hallucinations, yes," G. responded. "Why? What is making us see hallucinations? If we know this, maybe we can stop having hallucinations."

"Hypnotism," J. offered.

"Conditioning," suggested B.

"Yes," agreed G., "conditioning is a form of hypnosis. We must remember that some children immediately see the clothes, not the King; while some children immediately see the King, not the clothes. Why is this so?"

"Perhaps something happens at birth during the trip down the birth canal," suggested A.

"Nothing quite so complicated. You do not have the equipment to really know how to obtain the answer. Actually the answer is very simple, too obvious; always the purloined letter.

"There is a catalyst to all this, and the catalyst is usually of the same form in every kind of problem like this. We do not see the King right away. We can grind away our misperceptions little by little to penetrate the veil of hypnosis, if we continue to remember, no matter what we think we see, that the King is naked.

"This is the penetrating prayer: *No matter what I think I see, the King is naked.* Eventually we will see the King, although it may require many repetitions to see that it is true; to use this aid to vision in order to penetrate the phenomenal veil — the King's invisible clothes. It is sufficient to know what we are looking for, even though we do not yet see the King. All we need to know is that the King is naked."

"Would we recognize the King if we saw Him?" B. inquired.

"That is the next question," said G.,

"Would we recognize the King if we saw Him, or do we only recognize the Queen who envelops, blankets the King? The Queen is invisible, yet all we see is the Queen.

"The clothes are invisible, yet we see only the clothes. Can we tear our gaze from the clothes and put our gaze on the King, who is naked?

"We are hearing rumors of the existence of a great powerful Absolute Being living right in our midst, in front of our eyes, and yet we cannot see Him! Do you understand the irony of this? Do you know that all phenomenal events seem to support the visibility of the Queen?

"It is not just under special circumstances that the King is naked; the King is *always* naked. We can point to the King and say 'the King is not just naked now, He is *always* naked.'

"We see the King's clothes, but we do not see the King, but the King is naked. Is that a paradox? No, it is not. The King's clothes are invisible! Then why do I see the King's clothes, and not the King?

"There is not any easy way to see this. It requires use of the catalyst over a very long period of time; it requires *practice* to see the King.

"If you were an astronomer it would take a long time before you knew what you were looking at. Anyone can look at the stars but it takes *practice* to *see* the stars in a coherent formulation."

"Most people would not be able to do that alone although there are some who have done it," added J. "Someone must show you, there are very few people who can learn this by themselves."

"It requires perseverance and help," said G.

"There are books that show us what we are looking at," chimed in S.

"As I said," continued G. in a playfully severe tone, "it requires perseverance and help. So much for the help, now about the perseverance . . . "

After the group had stopped laughing, G. went on, "What do we know about the Shekinah and the Garden of Eden? The second Adam and Eve were expelled from the Garden of Eden. Remember that the Garden of Eden was as large as the whole universe, the whole world. That gives you a hint."

"That we are *in* the Garden of Eden?" questioned J.

"We are in exile from the garden — we see the King's clothes, not the King," replied G. "We have not gone anywhere;

was Adam. Who was not? The Shekinah was not. She is wrapped around the Tree of Life, and she turns it into the tree of splendor. She glitters, turning it into a tree of a million rainbows. And she is left to guard the garden.

"It is forbidden to *study* the Kabala; it is not forbidden to *know* the Kabala. It is forbidden to study the Book of Zohar; yet it is not forbidden to know the Book of Zohar. It is not forbidden to *know* the Kabala. It is forbidden to *study* it. It is forbidden to study the Sephiroth, the Tree of Life; it is not forbidden to know the Sephiroth. It is forbidden to study the Law; it is not forbidden to know the Law.

"On the other hand, it is not forbidden to study the Shekinah in minute detail, or to know the Shekinah, in the biblical sense.

"In fact, the reuniting of the Shekinah,

No matter what I think I see, the King is naked.

there is no where else to go. The Garden of Eden and the phenomenal world both appear in the same form.

"What do we know about the Garden of Eden? Are there any inhabitants? What do we know about the inhabitants of the Garden of Eden?

Suggested B., "We are still being seduced by the snake."

"Eve and Satan were definitely expelled from the garden," replied G., "so

called the Bride of God, with the King is the entire task of the People of Israel.

"So it is forbidden to make data into intellectual knowledge," stated J.

"We have data," said G., "but can never put it together in the right way without help. We must know *how* before we can *do*. Before we get data we must have something in which the data can take root.

"After a long time we begin to

understand that what we see is not really what it appears to be. We begin, after a long time, to really see that the King is naked.

"Why is the King wearing the Queen as clothes? Why? We hear rumors that the Queen is the ultimate accommodator. Of course she is; she is invisible. Do you understand what that means?

"I will show you the ultimate card trick, but I will need invisible playing cards..."

G. asked J. to name a card, and then he would show her the invisible card. G. continued, "I can do this indefinitely with invisible cards. If you really began to *see* the cards after a while..." The group burst into laughter at the absurdity of this idea, and then stopped laughing when he added, "that would correspond more or less to your present conditioning now.

"The King is right here; we are a hair's breadth away from the Garden of Eden. Why can we not see the Garden of Eden?"

"We do not know how to look for it?" guessed L.

"You know now how to look for the King," replied G., "Why not look for the garden the same way? We are one hair's breadth from the Kingdom of Heaven, a hair's breadth from the Garden of Eden, a hair's breadth from the Eternal World. We are *in* it, yet *not* in it. We are liberated, yet we do not know it."

"As Mephistopheles said on the occasion of his conjuration by the good Doctor Faustus, 'Why, Faustus, this *is* Hell, *nor am I out of it.* Of all the inhabitants of Hell, none but Lucifer knows that Hell *is* Hell'."

ITEM

PHENOMENAL PHACT SHEET

Fenomenal Fact Sheet

PHENOMENAL FACT SHEET

FENOMENAL FACT SHEET

Dear Reader transformed to Deer Reeder

**********WELCOME TO**********
*****CAMP NON-PNENFOMENAL****

Dress requirements: No artificial outer skin is to be worn in the camp.

Campers are to remember at all times that everything they see in Camp Non-Phenomenal is a magical instrument, not an ordinary object, and therefore treat it accordingly. Magical instruments which have been contaminated by dirty phenomenal counterparts must be left outside the campgrounds.

If it becomes necessary to refer to the phenomenal during camp hours preface the statement or question with "Simon says . . . " as in "Simon says this is an ashtray."

Remember that all phenomena is illusion.

Remember that all movement is illusion.

In this camp everything is upside down. "I am sitting on my head on the ceiling" is one of the evocations we repeat to remember this.

The camp director has been in your dreams; do not be alarmed, he is your friend, lie flat on your back and do exactly as he says.

During camp activities keep in mind that it is better to be wrong than to guess. Whether your answer is wrong or a guess does not affect your raw score, but the quality of a wrong answer is higher than the quality of a guess. It is like the difference between a C and a C+, you get a C+ for trying but being wrong . . . but not *too* rong!

This is a legal camp, we therefore behave lawfully and are subject to higher Laws, such as the Law of Hospitality. For example, if food is offered we must eat, even though it will bring us, at least temporarily, back to the phenomenal.

The camp counselors are referred to as 'Saint' followed by their name, since they are invariably angels, celestial or infernal.

Involuntary trips into the phenomenal during camp hours will be subtracted from your score.

The Healing Service

The *New American Book of the Dead* is a powerful agent for the invocation of Angelic Healing Entities. Over the past seven years, we have received hundreds of reports of amazing successes in spiritual healing using this book. Now for the first time, we have included a simple, practical healing method which anyone can use.

The actual mechanism of healing is quite simple. The Reader does not heal the sick person. Healing is accomplished by reminding the non-phenomenal, spiritual self of its true relationship with the phenomenal, organic body. The reading acts as an invocation of an Angelic Entity which descends and performs the healing, helping the spiritual self to heal the phenomenal, organic self.

The function of the Reader is analogous to a midwife at bedside during childbirth. The midwife simply assists in the birthing process. In the same way, the Reader provides the readings which establish the correct relationship of the spiritual self and the organic body, and which invoke the Angelic Healing Entity.

An important key to the proper use of readings in the Healing Service is to learn relaxation as described in the chapter *Draining Exercise* given later in the book. When the body is relaxed, the Reader can more easily observe the play of mood and thoughts, making the healing readings easier and the contact stronger. The path of prayer opens because the Reader's mood is no longer subjective and personal, dictated by the artificial tension in the muscles.

Use of colored glass votive jars or colored candles to vibrate sympathetically with the non-phenomenal world is another key to successful healings. The Reader should mentally direct the colored light which radiates from the votive jar in a concentrated ray toward the part of the body which is affected by illness.

The Healing Service of the *New American Book of the Dead* is a very useful and effective way of service to others — family, friends and acquaintances.

Arrangements for the Healing Service

1. The Healing Service is performed twice daily. Suggested times for readings are 6 AM and 6 PM, although other times are often chosen to fit in with the Reader's schedule. Select times when you are able to read consistently at the same hour each day if you intend to perform the Healing Service for more than one day. The Healing Service is generally continued until the sick person begins to recover. As a rule, Healing Services last from 2 or 3 days to a week or two.

2. If possible, do your readings with the sick person in the room, or obtain a photograph of that person. The photograph should be wrapped in a light-proof container.

3. The set-up of the physical space is the same in all respects as for Transit readings. A votive jar of the color corresponding to the Brilliant Radiation for this Healing Service should be placed on the table in front of the photo stand. Choose the correct color of votive jar by turning to the Healing Reading and determining the Cleansing Radiation. To perform all Healing Services you will need seven different colored votive jars: violet, blue, white, green, yellow, red and orange.

4. To perform a Healing Service it is necessary to know the illness of the individual being healed. When you have that information, you can consult the *List of Common Diseases and Their Angelic Healing Entities* at the end of this section to learn the appropriate Healing Service. If the ill person is suffering from more than one illness, then you must decide which illness should take precedence, or do a double reading. This is not intended to take the place of competent medical attention.

The Healing Service Procedure

This general procedure is for all Healing Services. As you become familiar with the healing space and gain confidence in your abilities, you may wish to make some modifications which will help you achieve better contact.

1. Find a quiet place where you can properly relax as described in the chapter *Draining Exercise* given later in the book.

2. The reading space should be set up. Light the incense and the candle from the colored votive jar corresponding to the Brilliant Radiation (the Healing Ray). Take the photograph out of its lightproof container and place it on the photo stand.

Healing is accomplished by reminding the non-phenomenal, spiritual self of its true relationship with the phenomenal, organic body.

---

3. Begin the Healing Service with the following address to the Being:

"This Healing Service is directed to the Being of _____ (name of individual being healed) who is suffering from _____ (disease). May this Healing Service be used for the benefit of the Being of _____ (name) and for the healing and balancing of his (or her) organic body."

4. Now read the appropriate reading for the Chamber associated with the illness of the individual being healed

(selected from the *List of Common Diseases*). If you feel it is necessary read this several times through.

5. Close the Healing Service with:

"This completes the Healing Service for the Being of _____ (name of individual being healed). May this be used for the benefit of the Being and for the balancing and healing of his (or her) body."

While performing the Healing Service, you should, if possible, continue to monitor the physical condition of the sick person maintaining contact with him or someone close to him.

*   *   *

List of Common Diseases and Their Angelic Healing Entities

Disease: Angel	Chamber
Acne: *Ithuriel*	4
Anemia: *Sariel*	27
Apnea: *Azza*	30
Apoplexy: *Adririon*	10
Asthma: *Hadriel*	7
Baldness: *Anafiel*	6

Disease: Angel	Chamber
Bladder diseases: *Zadkiel*	2
Bilious attacks: *Emmanuel*	3
Bright's disease: *Zadkiel*	2
Bronchitis: *Barakiel*	15
Cancer: *Ashruliel*	11
Cataract: *Kemuel*	16
Catarrh: *Abraxis*	40
Colera: *Sabriel*	12
Colic: *Emmanuel*	3
Colitis: *Emmanuel*	3
Common cold: *Hadraniel*	5
Concussion: *Israfel* Clear Light I or 32	
Constipation: *Ashtoreth*	49
Consumption: *Hadriel*	7
Cuts and burns: *Azbugah*	14
Cystitis: *Araquiel*	35
Deafness: *Shemuel*	26
Diabetes: *Ashruliel*	11
Diarrhea: *Uriel*	31
Dyspepsia: *Emmanuel*	3
Earache: *Shemuel*	26
Eczema: *Ithuriel*	4
Epilepsy: *Phanuel*	22
Eye troubles: *Kemuel*	16
Faulty elimination: *Ashtoreth*	49
Fevers: *Sakhriel*	9
Flatulence: *Emmanuel*	3
Flu (influenza): *Sakhriel*	9
Gallstones: *Tagriel*	8
Gastritis: *Emmanuel*	3
Goiter: *Adririon*	10
Gout: *Azbugah*	14
Headaches: *Shekinah*	46
Heart complaints: *Shekinah*	46
Hepatitis: *Sabriel*	12
High blood pressure: *Shekinah*	46
Hoarseness: *Barakiel*	15
Hysteria: *Penemu*	37
Inflammation of the ovaries: *Lilith*	44

Disease: Angel	Chamber
Insomnia: *Azazel*	36
Jaundice: *Sabriel*	12
Kidney diseases: *Zadkiel*	2
Laryngitis: *Barakiel*	15
Leprosy: *Ithuriel*	4
Lumbago: *Azbugah*	14
Measles: *Araquiel*	35
Menopausal problems: *Lilith*	44
Menstration, excessive: *Lilith*	44
Mental disorders: *Phanuel*	22
Mumps: *Araquiel*	35
Muscle spasms: *Azbugah*	14
Nausea: *Emmanuel*	3
Nervous ailments: *Penemu*	37
Palpitations: *Shekinah*	46
Paralysis: *Adirion*	10
Parasites, skin: *Chayyiel*	17
Placenta previa: *Lilith*	44
Pleurisy: *Hadriel*	7
Pneumonia: *Hadriel*	7
Psoriases: *Ithuriel*	4
Rheumatism: *Azbugah*	14
Sciatica: *Azbugah*	14
Sexual diseases: *Lilith*	44
Shock: *Israfel*	Clear Light I or 32
Sinusitis: *Abraxis*	40
Skin diseases: *Ithuriel*	4
Sore throat: *Barakiel*	15
Spinal meningitis: *Adririon*	10
Spleen infections: *Shekinah*	46
Stings: *Azbugah*	14
Thrombosis: *Shekinah*	46
Thyroid trouble: *Adririon*	10
Ulcers: *Azbugah*	14
Uteri lepsis (falling womb): *Lilith*	44
Varicose veins: *Azbugah*	14

ITEM

Healing Service Case Histories

The following accounts are from individuals who have successfully used the *American Book of the Dead* for healing purposes. Some have had various phenomena occur while the reading was happening, such as tingling at the back of the neck, space changes, or certain emotions arising spontaneously. The following accounts will provide insight into how others have used the Healing Service . . .

J. F., of Tucson, Arizona writes about a Healing Service he performed for a woman who had an abdominal growth:

"I was using the *American Book of the Dead*, reading the Healing Service both morning and evening, at the same time every day, for a woman who was in the hospital having an abdominal growth biopsy-tested for malignancy. As soon as I heard of her troubles, I started reading the Healing Service . . . focusing my concentration on her abdomen. There was a very clear image of the size of the growth and its texture.

"After three days of Healing readings I got a call. The woman said that the growth had shrunk in size and that it was not cancerous. She was released from the hospital the next day and told to come back for a checkup in a week. I continued the readings. When she went back for testing, the growth had miraculously disappeared. I did not feel that I was responsible for the miracle but merely played my part as reader."

R. P., of Philadelphia, Pennsylvania writes about doing Healing Services for a friend's father who had hepatitis:

"The Healing Service from the *New American Book of the Dead* was very effective for my friend's father who had a severe case of hepatitis. I read for a full week and there was marked improvement in his condition. He is now recuperating at home. I have decided to continue reading for him. This time I will do the Healing Service with my friend's father at his home. It gives me great satisfaction to know that through the healing readings I may be of service to others.

"I experienced a certain kind of phenomena while doing this healing reading. I was able to tell that I had made good contact because when I used the photograph it appeared three-dimensional. The thin frame of white around the picture sat still, while the picture inside wavered a bit. It appeared as if I was looking through a window and the photo was alive. He almost winked at me. I felt that he was going to talk to me any moment.

"I also experienced a tingling at the back of the neck, the sides of the head, and all the way up to the top of my head."

B. N., of Los Angeles, California writes about reading for an uncle who was experiencing severe depression and paralysis of his legs:

"While living on the East Coast two years ago I got to know my husband's family. His uncle, an older man in his 70's, was the family patriarch. Some months after I first met him, I had a very special talk with him on Thanksgiving. I felt I made a good connection with him, and if I needed to I could send a message to him telepathically.

"A couple of months later he was in the hospital and his legs just wouldn't move. He couldn't stand on them any more. Having had the talk with him at Thanksgiving, and then talking with him again in the hospital, I could tell he was losing his will to live.

"My husband and I began to read for him, focusing our attention on his legs and the whole of his body. After a week my husband asked his father how his uncle was doing. He told us that while he was visiting the hospital the uncle had said, 'I want you to thank Mark for calling me. That was really great of him to do that.'

"Mark's father asked if he had indeed called his uncle. Mark told him that he hadn't, but we had been saying some prayers for him.

"Shortly after that we learned that his legs had healed and he could walk again. The doctors said that they didn't know why he could suddenly stand on his legs. They said he was old and psychologically depressed. After the Healing Service his will-to-live was reactivated."

B. K. of Ottawa, Canada writes about a direct link-up with an extremely ill patient throughout a long and very difficult operation. A 90-year-old man slipped and broke his hip while getting out of the shower, and he was given only a very slim chance of recovery:

"My friend phoned about 7 AM to say that her grandfather from Chicago was in the emergency ward and was scheduled for the operating room at 9 AM. The doctors were all very pessimistic about his chances of recovery because he was 90 years old and needed to have a pin put in his hip. Because of the seriousness of the operation and recovery, a continuous Healing Service was started. My friend, Mary, rushed over a large photo of her grandfather, and I began the Healing Service immediately.

"As soon as I started reading for her grandfather, a powerful contact was achieved. There were dramatic space changes, the colors in the room became much brighter, and his photo seemed alive. I could see the hip that was broken, so I directed my energy and attention to that spot. As the contact got stronger I could see his chest rising and falling with his breathing by watching the photo. During the 4-hour operation, I was kept informed of all of his vital signs, as I continued the reading without a break.

"The doctors were amazed at how well my friend's grandfather did. One of them even commented, 'He went through the operation like a 20-year-old.' I continued the Healing Service for a week. By the end of the service, he was home and recuperating at a very rapid rate."

INSTRUCTIONS
for the
VOYAGER

Introduction to the Transit Experience

Because it is a continuing reverberation of organic phenomena, Transit looks just like ordinary life. Familiar people — relatives, friends, the neighborhood pharmacist, a pet dog or cat, the telephone, sounds of passing automobiles are all possible phenomena of Transit.

Habits of the phenomenal self transform the non-phenomenal eternal world of pure light in endless extension into ordinary organic world phenomena. Remember: *the nature of the phenomenal world is phenomena. All* phenomena — not just some phenomena — is illusion. That means everything we think we see, hear, smell, touch, taste, have a conversation with . . . or read.

Unfortunately, organic consciousness usually does not include control over organic habits, particularly the habit of making hallucinations of organic-world phenomena when confronted with the absence of phenomena.

A Voyager who is not *organically trained* to function without phenomena will go into 'blackout' and wake up only after it is all over. If we have trained only the mind, when it dissipates we will be subject to the force of organic-world phenomenal reverberations, which lead inevitably to automatic organic rebirth.

The inner game of dying requires discipline. In a culture which has a taboo against death, this means overcoming many deeply ingrained social and personal superstitions.

We may enter and leave the non-phenomenal world *at any time* for periods of seconds, minutes, hours, or years, and be reborn into the phenomenal world *at any time* with *any* size, shape, age and subjective identity.

the nature of the phenomenal world is phenomena.

Unless we have had training in organic sensing, it will be as if *nothing unusual had happened.* We will take rebirth unknowingly.

Once in rebirth, we will insist that our *memories, interests* and *body* are the same we've always had! After all, if we had been in the non-phenomenal and then expelled back into the phenomenal, we would *know* it — *wouldn't we?*

If you have not had any training in the feeling and sensing exercises and you are in doubt about whether you are in Transit or not, here are some suspicious places to look. The chances are very good that you are in Transit if you find yourself:

In a bus or train or plane or any other form of public 'transportation'. Compulsively walking from room to room in a house or apartment and you cannot stop moving. In a small room or trailer with one other person whose face keeps changing subtly, as if the light is shifting.

Alone for long periods of time. In an older hotel room or motel room. Continually going into a bathroom or kitchen, or back and forth from bathroom to kitchen. Waking up suddenly from a 'nightmare', or a dream about yourself having a different body.

Driving in a car for a long period of time. Watching a clock that moves impossibly slowly. In an older theatre with balconies and basement, watching a film that seems familiar to you but you cannot remember having seen before — usually the film will have an unusual amount of senseless violence or seem very religious.

Getting a phone call in the middle of the night. Attending a funeral of 'someone else'. Lost either in a small town or a very large city. Playing with pictures or cards with pictures on them for an unusually long time, and you keep arranging the cards in different order. Inside a tunnel or going down escalators. In an elevator alone.

Once in rebirth, we will insist that our *memories, interests* and *body* are the same we've always had!

Sitting in front of the television set, usually seated in either a cane chair, wicker chair, or rocking chair, generally of oak, with side arm rests.

Traveling a tube of water while surfing. Sitting alone in a room for a long time. Awakening after an unusually long sleep — a full day at least. Dancing to 'rock' music (the 'Rock' is another word for Basic Creation before the Cosmos was constructed).

Sitting or standing in the dark for a long time. Standing in front of a mirror for an unusually long time. In a city which, although large, appears to be abandoned or underpopulated. Having strange dreams about 'other worlds' or 'another life'.

'Dreaming' you had died or 'almost died'. Seeing people whom you had thought were long since dead on the street or in restaurants. Sitting in a caged area or in what appears to be a playpen for children (usually there will be red, blue, green, white and yellow lights just out of range).

Talking with mysterious strangers who stop you on a street or in a public place and begin speaking as if they know you. Feeling very tired and run-down although there is no apparent reason for it.

Feeling apprehension, as though something terrible is about to happen — a feeling of dread. Getting a new car or new clothes or moving to another house or town.

Getting divorced or married or changing partners. Changing friends or neighbors. Listening to loud music with lots of rumbling bass sounds in it or high-pitched tones which hurt your ears.

Going to recording studios or broadcast stations, either radio or TV. Leaving one country and going to another, or going from 'state' to 'state'.

Through the whole history of the universe every sentient life form has made this voyage. Whether you find heaven, hell or purgatory, at the worst you will take rebirth in the same ego-type you started with.

Here is a key: tap the nine-billion year old storehouse of cellular data contained in every cell of the body.

In the non-phenomenal world, the organic ego cannot function. The Voyager descends into lower states until he finds one in which he is able to function.

from room to room • • • back and forth
impossibly slowly • • • inside • • •sitting in front
of
in the dark • • • 'almost died' • • • tired and
run-down
getting • • • changing . . .
Through the whole history of the universe every
sentient life form has made this voyage.

Sensations at Transition and Expulsion

Sensations at Transition usually last from 60 to 90 seconds, and may come at regular 22-minute intervals.

Shakes, nausea, hiccups or sweat are common symptoms. They might cause discomfort but are normal at this time, along with feelings of restlessness, chills, backache, trembling thighs, irritability, weakness, vertigo.

Key: Concentration and Relaxation. Empty the mind of everything but slow and steady breathing. Do not try to intellectually direct the body.

Toward the end you may begin to think that you cannot keep your concentration on the readings, but you can . . . do not allow the luxury of self-pity or exhaustion. The exercises have increased your strength little by little, and now you are able to sustain your concentration and attention. When Expulsion occurs, the body may feel as if it is going to explode; just relax completely.

Vision changes radically during Expulsion; so does the connection to the body and environment. You may notice a gradual periodic change or become aware of it suddenly. Sound and other perceptions take on a distant quality.

During this transitional period from the phenomenal to the non-phenomenal, any feeling of exhaustion will leave suddenly; the Voyager will feel exhilarated, contented, fulfilled and happy.

Relaxation is essential between cycles of sensation. Conserve energy for Transition and Expulsion.

If the Voyager is not breathing properly one or all of these signs may develop:
—dizziness
—tingling sensation in arms and legs
—nausea
—hiccups
—burping
—vertigo, or loss of balance

You can try these remedies for hyperventilation:
— Cover the mouth with hands cupped and breathe the expelled air back in.
— Breathe into a brown paper bag.

What you are trying to do is to *increase* carbon dioxide and *decrease* oxygen to counteract the effect of hyperventilation.

Transition:

Transition means simply to pass from the state of phenomenal perceptions to the state of non-phenomenal perceptions. This is the midpoint.

Keep eyes open in good eye-to-eye contact if possible. Maintain contact and breathe together following the flow of the Voyager's breathing, providing a stable focal point for the rhythm of breath. Agree beforehand on what your signals mean!

Expulsion:

The actual passage out of the phenomenal world begins.

Sensations will occur in periods of 60 to 90 seconds, lasting 60 to 90 seconds in each wave. This should occur approximately 10 - 20 times, then cease completely, as the body is subdued by waves of cleansing radiation as one moves farther from the world of phenomena.

Usually it takes several tries to find the right way to move out of the phenomenal body. Perceptions may become dim for a few moments until the non-phenomenal vision establishes itself.

Draining Exercise

Relaxation ought to be the most natural action we can perform, yet very few people really know how to relax completely.

Most people try to relax by calming their mind and emotions, but they cannot be calmed directly. Thought and emotion follow the state of the body and can be directed by altering the body's state, so if we can get the body to relax, our inner functions will go along with it to accommodate to the whole state.

In this way we can actually select moods and whole trains of thought for ourselves, provided we know how to orchestrate and choreograph the body's postures, gestures and tempo of activity.

Keeping the facial mask totally relaxed, place your attention on the feet, directing them mentally to release all tension until they remain motionless in a lazy kind of 'voluntary paralysis'.

Then move the attention upward along the legs, directing them to release any tension they may have been holding. As the body is lying down on its back at this point, there is no reason to maintain tension in the legs, is there?

Then move the attention upward along the legs to the thighs, directing them in the same way to release all tension that was used to maintain the body's balance when standing. Feel gravity take hold of the body and press it downward toward the couch or bed.

Now just for a moment return the attention to the feet to see that tension has not in the meantime crept back in while your attention was elsewhere. We will do this periodically as we direct the body to release tensions, checking those areas already 'pacified', as is said in military operations.

Bringing the attention farther upward to the abdomen, direct the abdominal wall muscles to release tension which they have been maintaining, then check the facial mask to see that it is still relaxed.

The facial mask serves as the director for the rest of the body. If it is tense, so is the whole body; if it is relaxed, then the body can also be directed to relax. We can, with a little practice, learn to keep the whole body relaxed by monitoring the tension of the facial mask.

Bring the attention quickly up to the chest and direct the chest and back muscles to release tension, waiting for them to do so before moving on to the neck and shoulder muscles.

Remind yourself that it is not necessary to tense up the facial mask in order to dramatize mood or character.

When the body is relaxed, the Voyager can easily observe the play of mood and thoughts, making the reading easier by opening the path of suggestion, and if trust has developed between the Voyager and Reader, the Voyager can be moved gently through the major events of Transit without tension building up artificially because of habitual muscle interference.

Contact Exercise

The Reader and Voyager face each other about two feet apart, holding eye contact without drifting off, becoming bored, laughing, giggling, frowning, and so forth.

The facial mask should be maintained at full relaxation, monitoring it periodically to check for any unknown tension which may have built up.

At first many types of phenomena will appear over the face, but continue the exercise until you can easily be with one another without having to dramatize social expressions and personality.

At first this may be uncomfortable or embarrassing, but that should tell you all the more that there is a good reason to continue this; social conditioning must be removed, and the tensions of the facial mask are the very first, and the least powerful, of these.

Along with the disappearance of the habit to express personality and social graces through the facial mask, some beliefs and considerations of social conditioning may disintegrate; that is all right — let them go.

Beneath social conditioning is a very strong set of inhibitions — against mayhem, murder and other violent actions against others. This deeper layer of behavior will not interfere with Transit material, and should be allowed to maintain itself.

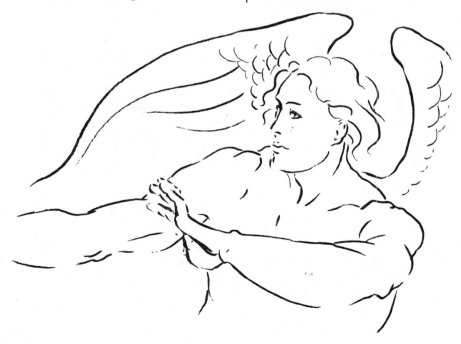

Breathing Exercises For Transition

Abdominal Breathing:

This is used during the early stages of Transition when tension or pain is not too strong. It is continued as far into Transition as is possible until 'accelerated breathing' becomes necessary to control sensations.

The breath moves in and out slowly, with a definite and controlled rhythm.

The facial mask is relaxed and the abdomen is allowed to rise and fall gently and slowly in cycles of five seconds for inbreath and five seconds for outbreath.

Day by day this periodic cycle can be increased to as much as thirty seconds for inbreath and thirty seconds for outbreath, provided the breathing follows the natural tempo of the organism.

A gentle gradient of five seconds more every three days should make this exercise safe and effective. Unless the time is built up slowly, however, this type of breathing can cause serious organic problems.

Use a 'cleansing breath' before and after each type of special breathing pattern. *A 'cleansing breath' is just a deep inhaling breath, letting the air out naturally for the exhalation in a gentle whooshing sound through the open mouth,* not with closed mouth where the outbreath is expelled through the nostrils.

Accelerated Breathing:

This is the Key Method of controlled breathing for transcending stress, pain and shock — even the shock resulting from accident. It is the primary technique for easy Transition if it is properly mastered.

Using a flute-type set of the mouth, allowing the cheeks to catch and rebound most of the expelled carbon dioxide in the outbreath, hyperventilation cannot occur and breathing is effortless.

Incorrect formation of the mouth muscles could result in exhaustion and hyperventilation so practice is very necessary to eliminate incorrect breathing technique. As with all breathing exercises, it is always best to learn this directly from a coach who can correct mistakes before they become serious problems.

The rhythm of this breath is *cha-cha-cha* for the outbreath. The final short outbreath comes from the chest, not the abdomen, and is expelled a little more sharply than the first two, as if one is blowing across the mouth of a glass bottle to make a sound.

A gentle inbreath is taken between cycles of outbreath. Maintaining a comfortable rhythm with this breath is very important. Do not exaggerate the breath or force it.

With increased sensation or pain the force of the outbreath can be increased somewhat; however, when increasing the force of the outbreath, the mouth's opening should be tightened and decreased to compensate.

Sensation, especially pain, occurs in definite cycles. With increased sensation the force of the breath can be increased, then reduced when the cycle of pain is over. Crescendos of sensation generally become shorter as Transition is approached.

Pinching Exercise

Lie down on the back and take a cleansing breath. The Reader works as coach in this exercise; the coach pinches the muscle just behind the knees, slightly to the inside of the kneecap.

When the coach pinches the correct muscle, you will know it.

During the pinch, which is held for twenty seconds rather gently, then increased to a full pinch for twenty seconds, then a lighter pinch for another twenty seconds, the Voyager practices accelerated breathing to overcome and control the sensation.

Tears may come to the eyes. This is all right, but common sense must be used, as with all exercises.

The accelerated breathing is correctly performed when the sensation of the pinch becomes tolerable. This is a good test for correctness of the accelerated breath, as well as good preparation for high levels of pain and discomfort.

After the full sixty seconds of pinching which is broken into three parts of twenty seconds each, the coach releases the muscle and the Voyager takes a cleansing breath just as at the beginning of this cycle.

Example:

Coach says "Take a cleansing breath. A pain cycle is about to begin."

There is a twenty second light pinch, then a harder pinch for twenty seconds, then a lighter pinch . . . Accelerated breathing is increased and decreased to accommodate the increase and decrease in sensation. "All right, it's over. Take a cleansing breath."

Voluntary Passage

Passage from the phenomenal world can be voluntary when it is recognized as the cessation of wandering through the phenomenal world.

Voluntary passage can be achieved when we have thoroughly drilled ourselves *organically* and *emotionally* for the hallucinations which follow separation from the organic body and the absorption of the organic ego into the all-embracing endlessness of the non-phenomenal world. The technique of voluntary passage is the key to resurrection in more useful incarnations.

Life consists of a succession of incarnations; an *incarnation* is defined as, literally, *in-carne,* or 'in-the-flesh'. In its most useful sense, this definition could be stated as: The attention of the source-of-personal-attention is rooted, usually involuntarily, in the perceptions and sensations of the world of phenomena.

This universe is neither the first nor the last; it is only one in an infinite series of phenomenal formations, disappearing and reappearing in new forms, through which we pass continually until we finally decide to liberate ourselves from the cycle of death and rebirth, and our involvement with the drama of the phenomenal world, called 'The Wandering'.

Death dissolves the ego-complex, just as rebirth concentrates and forms it. Voluntary Expulsion and passage transcends the phenomena-hungry ego-complex, transferring identity to a simpler form of non-phenomenal ego which is unaffected by the process of dying and passage through Transit.

Preparation is the keystone to voluntary passage. Familiarity with the sights and sounds of the non-phenomenal world, such as the humming, rolling thunder and crackling noises which sometimes last for twelve hours after Expulsion, and events which seem to violate the laws of the phenomenal world, can overcome the disorientation which usually follows Expulsion from the organic body.

A prepared Voyager can easily transfer identity from the phenomenal to the non-phenomenal world and back again, entering deliberately into rebirth, accommodating to the organic matrix just as a key can be fitted to a lock.

If this transference is successful, there is no break of consciousness, although a momentary passage through the Primary Clear Light, in which all events are as-if-nonexistent, is inevitable.

At Expulsion, the sense of independent personal identity is dissolved. The reverberation of phenomenal consciousness lingers, and so the first and second stages of Transit are experienced. These reverberations of phenomenal consciousness begin about fifteen minutes after organic Expulsion.

The identity which remains is a pure, simple 'presence' — the real 'I' when we say 'I' — about which nothing more can be said than *I Am* . . . Anything beyond this is hallucination . . . *all* phenomena is illusion.

The remaining 'I', or real identity, expands into a clear and colorless light — for want of a better description — which is formless and empty, and which, for this reason, is called 'the Void', or 'the non-phenomenal world'.

When phenomenal consciousness dissipates, the elemental non-phenomenal world is unveiled. We say we are 'out-of-body'.

The non-phenomenal world is the absence of all hallucination.

The Limitless Entity which is bodiless and without aspect is the 'Knower'. To be able to remain impartially in the non-phenomenal world without fear, loss or yearning for objects and sensations of the phenomenal world, is to attain 'Knower's Ark' — the Posture of Liberation, the practice of which is called 'meditation'.

The root causes of yearning for the phenomenal world are: pride, jealousy, apathy, anger, greed and lust. All phenomenal experiences in Transit are hallucinations caused by continuing reverberations of organic life, but hallucinations with sensations are real enough for the Voyager.

We do not lose our organic habits when we pass from the phenomenal world. They become our guiding force, pushing us this way and that through Transit states, forming our thoughts and emotions into what we expect to see . . . and most importantly, what we fear most, and have been avoiding by hiding in the world of phenomena.

In the same way that an ordinary psychological dream will suggest experiences, in Transit we can easily imagine ourselves going about our ordinary daily business. We can experience this solid three-dimensional color hallucination in life right now. We never really experience a 'real' world because we focus on the phenomenal coating of the world, not the real world itself. We see the invisible clothes of the King, but we do not — and under ordinary conditions cannot — see the King.

The technique of voluntary passage is the key to resurrection in more useful incarnations.

The events of Transit are no less substantial than the events of ordinary human life. If we are in the habit of returning to work every morning, our first

All phenomena is illlusion.

impulse in Transit is likely to be, "Who's minding the store?"

Usually by the time we realize that we have passed from one world and are going to be reborn in another, it is too late; we are already on the road to rebirth. We could say we have the habit — we are addicted to — the organic world. We are *phenomenal junkies*.

The attention of the source-of-personal-attention is rooted, usually involuntarily, in the perceptions and sensations of the world of phenomena.

The Transit body of the untrained Voyager is similar to the organic emotional body. It is a 'phantom body' in the same way that a man who has lost a leg is still able to sense his toes. In Transit we have sensations of a phantom body, although the organic body has been removed in the 'surgery of death'. This phantom body is called the *Body of Habits* because it is ruled by habit, not by mind or emotion. It is the body with which we will go through Transit.

Ordinarily we are conditioned by phenomenal life to fall into a random set of involuntary habits. The very idea of 'habit' means to us that something has become involuntary. In the same way, we never receive training in ordinary life — although we should — to bring the thinking and emotional parts of ourselves

into the voluntary, either. They all fall one by one into the involuntary-passive state. We are warned to really practice these ideas, not just read about them. We can, with serious practice, learn to recapture and remold habits which we have lost to the involuntary parts of ourselves . . .

In the first stage of Transit the Voyager encounters the Clear Light, which is to the universe what 'I' is to the body. This is the body of the 'collective consciousness'; the 'mystical body of Christ'; the non-phenomenal world; the Garden of Eden from which we are expelled when we make our usual sudden spasmodic moves as if we were still in the phenomenal world.

To the phenomenal self, steeped as it is in phenomenal world reverberations, nothing will seem out of place, because we have no logical apparatus with which to view and compare these events with phenomenal perceptions and experiences; we are blind to the non-phenomenal world — bulls in a china shop — wedding guests in street clothes — and are cast out.

To recognize and act accordingly within the non-phenomenal world is to achieve liberation. Liberation may or may not be permanent, according to deep-seated habits. Even the smallest yearning or attachment can draw us back unless we allow a cleansing process to take place, and we have trained our vision and manifestations to correspond to the non-phenomenal world. No matter how careful we are, if any vestige of karma — habits of the organic world — remains, sooner or later we will be expelled into rebirth in the phenomenal world where, according to our activities and reactions, we clearly belong . . .

Each of the lower worlds is a concentration of one or another of the 'poisons' . . . pride, jealousy, apathy, inattention, anger, greed and lust. The Angelic Guides will assume first the passive, and then the aggressive, forms of each of these primal emotional organic habits, because we are conditioned to project these on everything we see.

The 'I', or God, of our universe never destroys utterly; He draws His Body, the universe, into his Formless Self, just as we draw our material formations into our formless and colorless selves until just 'I' and *reverberations of phenomena* remain. In the phenomenal world we are clothed in form and even in the non-phenomenal world we tend to continue to relate to our environment in the same way.

clutch at every passing phenomenal projection, but allow the flow to continue unhindered by our desire for stability.

To be conscious in the real sense of the word is to be able to tolerate ever-flowing change, to accept all formations as they appear, and to know that all phenomena is illusion, within which is the real, non-phenomenal, world which we can train our vision to see, and our habits to conform to. We can learn not to bump clumsily into non-phenomenal walls . . . to housebreak ourselves in the non-phenomenal world.

At the end of the second stage, in which organic reverberations project themselves over the non-phenomenal world, one passes into the third stage in which rebirth becomes more attractive and inevitable. The previous life becomes dim and distant, although the same basic habits are retained for the next incarnation.

We focus on the phenomenal coating of the world, not the real world itself. We see the invisible clothes of the King, but we do not — and under ordinary conditions cannot — see the King.

The automatic periodic Expulsion from the phenomenal world can be terrifying to one who is habitually dependent on objects of the organic world. If we can form the habit of *consciousness without phenomena,* we are able to remain awake in this state. We must not cling and

The next rebirth is now visible by certain feelings and premonitions representing the first sign of fulfillment of habitual desires. The Body of Habits now accommodates itself to the world in which it will take rebirth, and in a way, the Body of Habits *becomes* the world of rebirth.

No single rebirth is eternal; all things must someday pass; no matter how seemingly permanent, we eventually find our way into a new world in which new habits must be adopted, or we are expelled and forced to return to the old.

---

we are
phenomenal junkies.

After rebirth the Voyager passes dreamily out of Transit into a state of organic consciousness, with the chance once again to make a voluntary Body of Habits which, without mind or emotions, can attain liberation by having the habit of liberation. This is why it is said, *liberation begets liberation.*

When we can take rebirth in a suitable matrix or essence-form, we are more able to achieve this. We can be prevented from forming a voluntary Body of Habits by taking rebirth in a form heavily controlled by involuntary, organic, habits — for example, in a family of Plymouth Brethren.

The best incarnation for the formation of a new Body of Habits is one which has no particular organic destiny, no real place in the phenomenal world; a misfit, an outcast — but with real skills and noncompetitive abilities. A rare combination, but essential in the struggle for liberation.

**to be able to tolerate
ever-flowing change
nchannnge
olerate tee
veverr-lowflowwing
abel-ll-lllL**

ITEM

Phenomenal Phact Quiz

All phenomena is illusion, except:

- ☐ Mom & Dad
- ☐ The children
- ☐ The new car
- ☐ The boss
- ☐ Cigarettes & coffee
- ☐ The mortgage
- ☐ Diarrhea
- ☐ The wrong end of a 12 gauge
- ☐ Death and taxes
- ☐ Relationships
- ☐ Duty
- ☐ Dirty dishes
- ☐ Independence & privacy
- ☐ Hunger
- ☐ Other (Please list)

_____
_____
_____
_____
_____
_____
_____
_____
_____
_____
_____
_____
_____
_____

First Stage Transit: Body Of Habits

At the moment of death, the Body of Habits is like a rubber ball. It has most energy at that time, so it bounces all the way 'up' into the Clear Light; depending on the amount of energy released at the moment of death, it can stay in the Clear Light for longer or lesser periods.

On the next bounce, it rises to the level of Violet Light. The Transit Body is traversing the light spectrum. At the bottom end, the Transit Body is shocked into a temporary oblivion. The Voyager may have periods of blackout interspersed with periods of exposure to the light-spectrum. The Voyager needs a reminder of where he is before he hits the top end of the cycle again.

First Bounce: CLEAR LIGHT. Depending upon the amount and quality of work done on the nervous system during human existence, penetration of this field will be greater or less. Then the down bounce into the area of oblivion. This down bounce may be viewed as a blackout area.

Second Bounce: VIOLET LIGHT. There is still enough energy to escape rebirth and to attain Liberation in the Clear Light. The light of the Animal Ego Formation, soft orange, is reflected light; the breakup into colors of the spectrum will cause harmonics after the disintegration of the tonic. Then the down bounce into oblivion once again, 'the Bottom of the Well'.

Third Bounce: BLUE LIGHT. The light of the Saintly Ego Formation, soft white, is reflected light. Then the down bounce again, not as deep as the first or second.

Fourth Bounce: WHITE LIGHT. Then the down bounce again, less deep than the previous three. Finally this bouncing up and down averages out, and there is no more death-transition energy with which to move around, forcing the Voyager to take rebirth in one of the Ego Formations in the middle of the visible spectrum.

All of the various hallucinations seen during Transit are simply the seven primal components of consciousness displaying themselves one at a time, then merged into a single manifestation. During First Stage Transit, the elements of consciousness are viewed as they exist in reality: implacable and unchanging.

Then in Second Stage Transit *reflections* of the primal components of

> The Voyager needs a reminder of where he is before he hits the top end of the cycle again.

consciousness, the 'left hand of God', appear. These components merge once again, which process is called 'The Play of Consciousness'. This creates the effect of realities, ego, awareness and existence. They form interlocking postures which determine the Voyager's new Ego Formation.

The specific consciousness which forms determines how the world — which objectively *never* undergoes change — will be viewed and understood. Rebirth is not re-entry into the world, but the formation of a new subjective phenomenal blanket over the eternal, non-phenomenal, world.

Once crystallized, the new consciousness cannot be altered except by a breakdown process such as Transit. Sometimes the reformed consciousness is even more securely conditioned than the previous one, and ego is strengthened rather than broken.

The experienced Voyager is able to maintain recognition that all phenomena is illusion and will be able to allow organic-phenomenal hallucinations to proceed without resistance. Ego demands and explanations can evoke a whirlwind of hallucination.

Energy can pattern itself to accommodate any image the Voyager conjures up — human, bestial, heroic, monstrous, robotic, grotesque — an endless procession of forms, sounds and personalities. The solution is always to recognize them as self-produced phenomena.

The solution is always to recognize them as self-produced phenomena.

ITEM

The Patchwork Quilt

G. asked, "Does anyone know of the crazy patchwork quilt?"

"The mantle of the dervish," J. suggested.

"Have you heard of quilting bees? Women sit in a circle making quilts. Where? Not in a barn or kitchen, but in church. Each lady would bring her patches to be added to the quilt. It was a community gathering.

"The patchwork mantle of a dervish, his robe, is a picture of God. This," G. paused sweeping his hand across to indicate the entire room and its contents, "is also a patchwork quilt, a picture of God. You will understand eventually; someday you may penetrate the patchwork with your vision and see God.

"The patchwork quilt was also a community project in the Middle East. The story of Joseph and his robe is a story from antiquity, from Biblical times, well known in the Middle East because of the allegory involved. Joseph's Robe of Many Colors was a patchwork quilt. The story reminded people to see God by viewing the blended form of the quilt as a whole thing-in-itself."

"G., you said earlier that we pass into the phenomenal world by imposing phenomena on the non-phenomenal world; is this right?" M. asked.

"Yes, that is right," G. said. "I can prove it to you. Where are you right now?"

"In a room," M. replied.

"You are in fact," G. clarified, "in the non-phenomenal world; but you do not know it. You are a hair's breadth from the Garden of Eden.

"We do not know, because we impose phenomenal habits, reactions, forms, and limits on the non-phenomenal world. When we are able to stop ourselves from habitually imposing phenomenal separation of forms on the non-phenomenal world, we pass directly into the non-phenomenal world. If we impose the phenomenal world on the non-phenomenal we either take rebirth or throw ourselves into a second-stage deterioration which also leads eventually to rebirth. In other words, we respond to the non-phenomenal with phenomenal reactions. Almost certainly this will occur within the first few minutes of exposure to the non-phenomenal world without the automatic buffer of phenomena.

"Does anyone know what a yantra is? A yantra is a visual meditation device. Imagine sitting before an abstract painting for several years. Eventually one will talk to it, and it will talk to you. One will see forms, hallucinations. What we are seeing right now is not three-dimensional. We are looking into a hollow sphere in which there are blotches of color and shape which suggest forms. After a while sheer *ennui* suggests movement and forms, then finally, significance.

"Imagine a hollow sphere made of a mirror, producing a total reflection. Now imagine that on the inside of the sphere are painted many fuzzy indistinct forms. Where the eyes on these figures would be, imagine just holes.

"Next, imagine an organism sufficiently large to cover, like a thin film, the entire sphere from the outside, which brings each of its myriad eyes to where each of the holes are in the sphere.

"Everything we see from one peripheral point to the other and from top to bottom is what we want to see. It is our subjective vision. If it did not seduce us into involvement then it would involve us through fear, sensation, passion or something else which would make us wish to become involved.

"When we can see both the phenomenal and non-phenomenal worlds voluntarily, we have achieved a certain balance, after which we can learn to work. Our viewpoint on what happens to us is very different after we have seen the angelic world and understood what we have seen. On our voluntary return to the phenomenal, we are able to understand the forces which move us, and perhaps take a more voluntary part in the wonderful cosmic dance of which we are each a vital part."

First Stage Transit: The Clear Light

To maintain Clear Light as long as possible, the prepared Voyager will let events flow without control or direction. One phenomenon of the Secondary Clear Light is rhythmic throbbing pulsations of the Transit Body, sensed as a whole.

There may be sounds of crackling, pounding and whooshing, and sensations of melting, freezing and trembling.

If the Voyager fails to recognize and conform to the non-phenomenal world, the force of habit takes over and habitual phenomenal routine resumes, which forces Expulsion from the non-phenomenal world, and inevitable — and sometimes sudden — phenomenal-world rebirth.

Second Stage Transit: Identifying the Cleansing Radiation

The Voyager in the Second Stage of Transit perceives the Cleansing Radiations as a succession of pure brilliant colors, along with the softly glowing globes of the phenomenal worlds. Practice in everyday life will increase the ability to differentiate Cleansing Radiations, which offer release from phenomenal attachments, from the glowing embers of the phenomenal world, which seem to offer relief from the starkness of the non-phenomenal world.

Radiations are non-reflected sources of light. To shift the vision from reflected light to radiation, squint the eyes so that the vision penetrates into the shadows, in which the radiation, because it is not overwhelmed by reflected light in the ordinary spectrum, becomes easily visible.

This is an exercise to practice identifying Cleansing Radiation: Determine which is the brightest light to be found in your immediate surroundings. For example, you may see at first a light in the kitchen that seems brighter than any other. Perhaps it is — but do not accept the first light you see. Continue on into the next room.

In the dining room, there is a light on the desk, but realize that it seems bright only because the room is dark. Do not be fooled by a soft light that seems bright only when it cannot be compared directly.

The next light, a little brighter, still does not satisfy your search, so continue looking. You come to a brilliant light flooding the hall. It is undoubtedly the brightest light in the house. Let yourself bathe in the light as if it were Cleansing Radiation.

An individual training for passage through Transit may discover other situations in the ordinary phenomenal world in which he sees correspondences with the non-phenomenal.

Third Stage Transit: Selecting Ego-Rebirth

Characteristic of human existence are various fascinating varieties of physical or psychological quirks which may manifest themselves at this stage.

The chances of favorable rebirth are increased if the process is allowed to take its own natural course, without effort or struggle.

It is unwise to resist at this stage; the readings can help the Voyager regain the First Stage if about to be expelled into sudden rebirth.

Entities encountered now may seem pitiless, mocking, superior, mysterious.

Exotic sexual encounters are not unusual during the Third Stage. Choosing rebirth is a profound art and should not be viewed carelessly or hastily. All rebirth options should be viewed. Don't be impatient. Take the time to wisely select rebirth.

Use 'pre-selection lifetime scanning' to choose a good rebirth. Choose impartially, without attraction or repulsion. Make your re-entry into organic existence graciously and in good humor, however ironic it may seem.

Usually rebirth will be a choice of the lesser of several discomforting evils. No matter which organic form is chosen, they are all alike in one respect: you will never get out of any of them alive.

. . . the world will still be there WHEN you get back.

Complete impartiality ensures that a wise choice is made. Savor every moment. No need to rush . . . the world will still be there when you get back.

If you find yourself struggling to return to organic life, relax. Remember where you are.

THE READINGS

Instructions for the Transit Reading Cycle

The exact procedure for the Readings — the physical layout of the Reading chamber, scheduling the Readings and presentation of the Readings — is outlined in detail in the chapters entitled *Attending Transition* and *Readings After Expulsion.*

The Readings for First Stage Transit are read during the Vigil and for the first 3 days following Expulsion. Day 1 is the day of Expulsion.

- *The Symptoms, Transition* and *Clear Light I* are read on day 1.
- *The Symptoms* and *Transition* are read to the Voyager at the onset of the Symptoms of Transition.
- The *Clear Light I* Reading takes place in the hour following Expulsion from the organic form. *Clear Light I* is read either **3** times or **7** times.

All Readings subsequent to the Readings for day 1 are performed twice daily, in the morning and evening, as outlined in the *Recommended Procedure For Transit Readings* in the chapter entitled *Readings After Expulsion.*

- *Clear Light II* is read on day 2. *Clear Light II* is read either **3** or **7** times.
- *Clear Light III* is read on day 3. *Clear Light III* is read either **3** or **7** times.

Readings for Second Stage Transit begin on day 4. Each Reading is read once in the morning and once in the evening.

- *Disintegration* followed by the *First Hall* followed by the *First Chamber* is read on day 4.
- The *First Hall* followed by the *Second Chamber* is read on day 5.

  •

  •

- The *Second Hall* followed by the *Eighth Chamber* is read on day 11.

  •

  •

- The *Seventh Hall* followed by the *Forty-Ninth Chamber* is read on day 52.

Readings for Third Stage of Transit are done on day 53. Each Reading is read once in the morning and once in the evening.

- *Recognition Factors* followed by *Selecting Rebirth* is read on day 53.

FIRST STAGE

The Symptoms

Releasing myself from efforts to maintain myself, letting go, I fall back into Endless Crystal Waters, no objects, no identity.

Earth sinking into Water, melting downward, heaviness creeping upward, drawn into the ocean.

Water sinking into Fire, coldness overtakes me, fire consumes me, swallowing me up.

Fire sinking into Air, exploding outward, dispersing to the wind, blown to atoms.

Air extending into Light, no weight, no dimension, utter silence.

Where is my face? Sounds fade into silence, Endless Crystal Waters, rocked in stillness.

Falling into darkness, everything is calm, no breath, no pain, awakening in Light.

Transition

As I pass from the organic form of ego into the consciousness of the Void, I release myself from the duty To Maintain The Organic Ego.

I hear a voice as deep as a thousand rolling thunders, and the voice is not one voice but the voices of many:

"Hear, O Bornless One, the key of the Moment of Passage, the Vision of Absolute Truth:

"Passing from the phenomenal world of organic life, I am reborn in the non-phenomenal world, in which the primal elements of the organic ego separate into their pure forms, appearing as phenomena and hallucination.

"Unto each is granted the power of Voluntary Passage at the moment of Expulsion from the organic world and at every moment of Transition afterward.

"I recognize myself to be the central force of the Shimmering Endless Void of the non-phenomenal world. I am transformed and eternal. The bonds of the organic ego and the distractions and necessities of organic life are broken as I awaken in the Clear Light with the liberation of consciousness."

Clear Light I

I am the Voidness of the Void,
Infinite, Eternal, Uncreated.
There is no other,
I am the Bornless One.

Not the Void of Darkness,
Not the Void of Nothingness,
Not the Void of Nonexistence,
I am Endless Crystal Waters.

All phenomena is illusion;
What is not illusion?
No one thing more than another.

Appearing in the dream,
Emotion, thought, sensation . . .
Acting and reacting,
With or without my presence the play goes on.

Impartial to it all,
Neither attracted nor repelled,
Alert and watchful,
Not making any sudden moves,
My habits will carry me through.

Clear Light II

I am the Voidness of the Void,
Infinite, Eternal, Uncreated.
There is no other,
I am the Bornless One.

Not the Void of Darkness,
Not the Void of Nothingness,
Not the Void of Nonexistence,
I am Endless Crystal Waters.

All phenomena is illusion;
What is not illusion?
No one thing more than another.

Appearing in the dream,
Emotion, thought, sensation...
Acting and reacting,
With or without my attention the play goes on.

Impartial to it all,
Neither attracted nor repelled,
Alert and watchful,
Not making any sudden moves,
My habits will carry me through.

Clear Light III

I am the Voidness of the Void,
Infinite, Eternal, Uncreated.
There is no other,
I am the Bornless One.

Not the Void of Darkness,
Not the Void of Nothingness,
Not the Void of Nonexistence,
I am Endless Crystal Waters.

All phenomena is illusion;
What is not illusion?
No one thing more than another.

Appearing in the dream,
Emotion, thought, sensation . . .
Acting and reacting,
With or without my agreement the play goes on.

Impartial to it all,
Neither attracted nor repelled,
Alert and watchful,
Not making any sudden moves,
My habits will carry me through.

SECOND STAGE

Disintegration

This is the Intermediate State in which visions appear during the breaking apart of organic ego.

Even though I have fallen below the Primary, Secondary and Tertiary Clear Light of the First Stage, it is still possible to attain spontaneous liberation in the Second Stage.

My portion of food is given away,
The body prepared for return to the stream of organic
    life,
My room is swept and cleaned of my presence,
The faces of friends and relatives pass before my vision.

Death has come to the organic ego,
As to all organic forms.
I will not cling to the body,
Nor to identity.

Not clinging to the organic ego,
I am not forced to wander.

As the organic ego disintegrates
I see the subtle shimmering Light,
A luminous body of water extending endlessly,
A continuous stream of vibration,
Expanding and contracting at the same time.

From within myself comes a rumbling reverberation
Like the sound of a thousand rolling thunders.
It is my own sound, the sound of the Body of Habits.
It cannot harm me. The less I resist, the better.

I have been disoriented for a while, but now I know what
    is happening to me.
As I look around I see the forms of organic ego in a
    swirling uproar.
The phenomena I am about to see are the primal forms
    of organic ego separating into entities.

First Hall

In the First Hall, a thousand distractions assault the senses; a hundred trials begin, of pride, anger, passion, jealousy, hunger, thirst, identity, fear, confusion, inattention, dreams and visions.

All that seems precious must be relinquished, and all that which is regarded as trivial must be revealed as precious. In the First Hall, all wishes great and small are multiplied to infinite powers.

I have drunk the draft of wine in the First Hall, and I am lost to ordinary life. I no longer fear the guardians at the gates who threaten to devour me. Let them devour what they will; I am not subject to their hungers.

They can take nothing from me, because I have nothing. They can do nothing to me, because I am nothing. They have no power over me, because I care nothing for the things of their world. If all worlds were to be annihilated in an instant, it would mean as little to me as the blending of a flame within a blazing inferno.

In the First Hall, all dogma, all beliefs and all certainties of the phenomenal world cease to exist and they cannot be regained.

First Chamber

These are the instructions for the First Chamber of the First Hall of the Kingdom of Heaven.

As I experience the disintegration of my organic identity into the primal elements of consciousness in my passage through the eternal world, the tattered remnants of the world of matter surround me.

These apparitions of phenomena are my own evocations, emanating from my own primordial consciousness.

In the First Chamber of the First Hall, the phantom reverberations of organic life are consumed in thoughts of the organic mind, evoking illusions of the phenomenal world, and my attention is caught up in this distraction.

I remember the thoughts of the organic mind in my passage through the phenomenal world and, passing once again into the endless emptiness of the Void, these thoughts and images swirl upward in my consciousness. Not swept away by them into the magnetic force of sudden rebirth, I invoke the presence of the guardian of the First Chamber of the First Hall of Heaven, the angel Cassiel, the angel of solitude and tears, who shows the unity of all things in the Eternal World and the futility of all pursuits in the phenomenal world. He who is a ruling prince of the Order of Celestial Powers; the angel Cassiel I invoke.

Brilliant violet radiation emanates from his heart, penetrating and dissolving all reverberations of the organic mind. At the same time, the phantom after-images of the phenomenal world, bathed in soft, smoky orange light, seem to offer refuge from the cleansing radiation.

Not becoming engulfed in the seductive magnetic force of rebirth, I bathe in cleansing radiation, the brilliant violet light dissolving all reverberations of the organic mind.

Wandering in the phantom images of the organic world, may my non-phenomenal self be cleansed by the brilliant radiation of the angel Cassiel; may inexorable reality be my guide.

May I remain impartial to phenomena, free from organic thoughts, not expelled in sudden rebirth.

May the blessed angel Cassiel be my protector. May he bring me safely through the First Chamber of the First Hall which is his domain. May he help me to remember my non-phenomenal self.

Involved with thoughts of solid form,
Swirling in a hurricane of force,
Separating into primal elements,
Phenomena of motion.

Opening before me paths of flesh and blood,
Nothing there but misery and pain,
Serene and calm I wait in stillness and in silence,
Bathed in cleansing radiation.

Brilliant in the light of inner vision,
I see my ego struggling for breath,
Clinging tightly to the remnants of organic life,
Terrified to die.

Penetrating radiation,
Violet explosion from his heart to mine,
Another light, soft orange, near the first,
Seems to offer refuge to my soul.

Melting in vibrating fusion,
Dissolving my resistance,
I lose the force of my reactions,
Not attracted to the orange light.

Wandering alone, maintaining thoughts of body symptoms,
Bathed in cleansing radiation,
Surrendering myself
In endless crystal waters.

All phenomena is illusion,
Neither attracted nor repelled,
Not making any sudden moves,
My habits will carry me through.

Second Chamber

These are the instructions for the Second Chamber of the First Hall of the Kingdom of Heaven.

As I experience the disintegration of my organic identity into the primal elements of consciousness in my passage through the eternal world, the tattered remnants of the world of matter surround me.

These apparitions of phenomena are my own evocations, emanating from my own primordial consciousness.

In the Second Chamber of the First Hall, the phantom reverberations of the organic mind are consumed in thoughts of my organic identity, evoking illusions of the phenomenal world, and my attention is caught up in this distraction.

I remember the thoughts of my organic identity in my passage through the phenomenal world and, passing once again into the endless emptiness of the Void, these thoughts and images swirl upward in my consciousness. Not swept away by them into the magnetic force of sudden rebirth, I invoke the presence of the guardian of the Second Chamber of the First Hall of Heaven, the angel Zadkiel, who is called the righteous angel, the angel of benevolence, mercy and remembering, who is a chief of the Order of Dominations, one of the nine great rulers of the Citadel of Heaven, who is among the seven great angels who may remain standing in the Divine Presence of God; the angel Zadkiel I invoke.

Brilliant blue radiation emanates from his heart, penetrating and dissolving all reverberations of my organic identity. At the same time, the phantom after-images of the phenomenal world, bathed in soft, smoky white light, seem to offer refuge from the cleansing radiation.

Not becoming engulfed in the seductive magnetic force of rebirth, I bathe in cleansing radiation, the brilliant blue light dissolving all reverberations of the organic mind.

Wandering in the phantom images of the organic world, may my non-phenomenal self be cleansed by the brilliant radiation of the angel Zadkiel; may inexorable reality be my guide.

May I remain impartial to phenomena, free from organic thoughts, not expelled in sudden rebirth.

May the blessed angel Zadkiel be my protector. May he bring me safely through the Second Chamber of the First Hall which is his domain. May he help me to remember my non-phenomenal self.

Involved with thoughts of my identity,
Swirling in a hurricane of force,
Separating into primal elements,
Phenomena of dimension.

Opening before me paths of time and space,
Nothing there but misery and pain,
Serene and calm I wait in stillness and in silence,
Bathed in cleansing radiation.

Brilliant in the light of inner vision,
I see myself controlling destiny,
Clinging to the content of the mind,
Frozen memory.

Penetrating radiation,
Blue explosion from his heart to mine,
Another light, soft white, near the first,
Seems to offer refuge to my soul.

Melting in vibrating fusion,
Dissolving my resistance,
I lose the force of my reactions,
Not attracted to the soft white light.

Wandering alone, maintaining thoughts of ego,
Bathed in cleansing radiation,
Surrendering myself
In endless crystal waters.

All phenomena is illusion,
Neither attracted nor repelled,
Not making any sudden moves,
My habits will carry me through.

Third Chamber

These are the instructions for the Third Chamber of the First Hall of the Kingdom of Heaven.

As I experience the disintegration of my organic identity into the primal elements of consciousness in my passage through the eternal world, the tattered remnants of the world of matter surround me.

These apparitions of phenomena are my own evocations, emanating from my own primordial consciousness.

In the Third Chamber of the First Hall, the phantom reverberations of my organic identity are consumed in thoughts of organic fear, evoking illusions of the phenomenal world, and my attention is caught up in this distraction.

I remember the thoughts of organic fear in my passage through the phenomenal world and, passing once again into the endless emptiness of the Void, these thoughts and images swirl upward in my consciousness. Not swept away by them into the magnetic force of sudden rebirth, I invoke the presence of the guardian of the Third Chamber of the First Hall of Heaven, the angel Emmanuel, whose name means 'The Ineffable Presence of God is with us now'. He who appeared beside Sidras, Misac and Abednego in the fiery furnace and was their protector and the source of their strength; the angel Emmanuel I invoke.

Brilliant white radiation emanates from his heart, penetrating and dissolving all reverberations of organic fear. At the same time, the phantom after-images of the phenomenal world, bathed in soft, smoky black light, seem to offer refuge from the cleansing radiation.

Not becoming engulfed in the seductive magnetic force of rebirth, I bathe in cleansing radiation, the brilliant white light dissolving all reverberations of the organic mind.

Wandering in the phantom images of the organic world, may my non-phenomenal self be cleansed by the brilliant radiation of the angel Emmanuel; may inexorable reality be my guide.

May I remain impartial to phenomena, free from organic thoughts, not expelled in sudden rebirth.

May the blessed angel Emmanuel be my protector. May he bring me safely through the Third Chamber of the First Hall which is his domain. May he help me to remember my non-phenomenal self.

Involved with thoughts of anxious expectation,
Swelling upward from my hidden self,
Separating into primal form,
Illusion of phenomena.

Opening before me paths of fear and anger,
Nothing there but misery and pain,
Serene and calm I wait in stillness and in silence,
Bathed in cleansing radiation.

Brilliant in the light of inner vision,
I see myself wreathed in seething hate,
Offering no sympathy or help,
Tantalizingly superior.

Penetrating radiation,
White explosion from his heart to mine,
Another light, soft black, near the first,
Seems to offer refuge to my soul.

Melting in vibrating fusion,
Dissolving my resistance,
I lose the force of my reactions,
Not attracted to the light of smoky black.

Wandering alone in worlds of fear,
Bathed in cleansing radiation,
Surrendering myself
In endless crystal waters.

All phenomena is illusion,
Neither attracted nor repelled,
Not making any sudden moves,
My habits will carry me through.

Fourth Chamber

These are the instructions for the Fourth Chamber of the First Hall of the Kingdom of Heaven.

As I experience the disintegration of my organic identity into the primal elements of consciousness in my passage through the eternal world, the tattered remnants of the world of matter surround me.

These apparitions of phenomena are my own evocations, emanating from my own primordial consciousness.

In the Fourth Chamber of the First Hall, the phantom reverberations of organic fear are consumed in thoughts of organic jealousy, evoking illusions of the phenomenal world, and my attention is caught up in this distraction.

I remember the thoughts of organic jealousy in my passage through the phenomenal world and, passing once again into the endless emptiness of the Void, these thoughts and images swirl upward in my consciousness. Not swept away by them into the magnetic force of sudden rebirth, I invoke the presence of the guardian of the Fourth Chamber of the First Hall of Heaven, the angel Ithuriel, deputy of the Holy Sephiroth, who was sent by the archangel Gabriel to reveal Satan to Eve in the Garden of Eden and by whose touch was Satan revealed; the angel Ithuriel I invoke.

Brilliant green radiation emanates from his heart, penetrating and dissolving all reverberations of organic jealousy. At the same time, the phantom after-images of the phenomenal world, bathed in soft, smoky red light, seem to offer refuge from the cleansing radiation.

Not becoming engulfed in the seductive magnetic force of rebirth, I bathe in cleansing radiation, the brilliant green light dissolving all reverberations of the organic mind.

Wandering in the phantom images of the organic world, may my non-phenomenal self be cleansed by the brilliant radiation of the angel Ithuriel; may inexorable reality be my guide.

May I remain impartial to phenomena, free from organic thoughts, not expelled in sudden rebirth.

May the blessed angel Ithuriel be my protector. May he bring me safely through the Fourth Chamber of the First Hall which is his domain. May he help me to remember my non-phenomenal self.

Involved with thoughts of jealousy and competition,
Rising upward from my hidden self,
Separating into primal form,
Repulsively attractive.

Opening before me paths of lingering uncertainty,
Nothing there but misery and pain,
Serene and calm I wait in stillness and in silence,
Bathed in cleansing radiation.

Brilliant in the light of inner vision,
I see myself suspiciously distrustful,
Clinging to my every action,
Gnawing at my soul.

Penetrating radiation,
Green explosion from his heart to mine,
Another light, soft red, near the first,
Seems to offer refuge to my soul.

Melting in vibrating fusion,
Dissolving my resistance,
I lose the force of my reactions,
Not attracted to the soft red light.

Wandering alone in worlds of jealousy,
Bathed in cleansing radiation,
Surrendering myself
In endless crystal waters.

All phenomena is illusion,
Neither attracted nor repelled,
Not making any sudden moves,
My habits will carry me through.

Fifth Chamber

These are the instructions for the Fifth Chamber of the First Hall of the Kingdom of Heaven.

As I experience the disintegration of my organic identity into the primal elements of consciousness in my passage through the eternal world, the tattered remnants of the world of matter surround me.

These apparitions of phenomena are my own evocations, emanating from my own primordial consciousness.

In the Fifth Chamber of the First Hall, the phantom reverberations of organic jealousy are consumed in thoughts of organic self-pity, evoking illusions of the phenomenal world, and my attention is caught up in this distraction.

I remember the thoughts of organic self-pity in my passage through the phenomenal world and, passing once again into the endless emptiness of the Void, these thoughts and images swirl upward in my consciousness. Not swept away by them into the magnetic force of sudden rebirth, I invoke the presence of the guardian of the Fifth Chamber of the First Hall of Heaven, the angel Hadraniel, who is called the Majesty of God, at the sight of whom Moses was struck dumb with awe, whose voice penetrates and reverberates through all the chambers of the halls of Heaven when he proclaims the Will of God; the angel Hadraniel I invoke.

Brilliant yellow radiation emanates from his heart, penetrating and dissolving all reverberations of organic self-pity. At the same time, the phantom after-images of the phenomenal world, bathed in soft, smoky blue light, seem to offer refuge from the cleansing radiation.

Not becoming engulfed in the seductive magnetic force of rebirth, I bathe in cleansing radiation, the brilliant yellow light dissolving all reverberations of the organic mind.

Wandering in the phantom images of the organic world, may my non-phenomenal self be cleansed by the brilliant radiation of the angel Hadraniel; may inexorable reality be my guide.

May I remain impartial to phenomena, free from organic thoughts, not expelled in sudden rebirth.

May the blessed angel Hadraniel be my protector. May he bring me safely through the Fifth Chamber of the First Hall which is his domain. May he help me to remember my non-phenomenal self.

Involved with thoughts of vanity and arrogance,
Towering above myself in pride,
Separating into primal form,
Immovably secure.

Opening before me paths of isolation,
Nothing there but misery and pain,
Serene and calm I wait in stillness and in silence,
Bathed in cleansing radiation.

Brilliant in the light of inner vision,
I see myself inferior and foolish,
Holding tightly to the past and present,
Terrified to bend.

Penetrating radiation,
Yellow explosion from his heart to mine,
Another light, soft blue, near the first,
Seems to offer refuge to my soul.

Melting in vibrating fusion,
Dissolving my resistance,
I lose the force of my reactions,
Not attracted to the soft blue light.

Wandering alone in worlds of pride,
Bathed in cleansing radiation,
Surrendering myself
In endless crystal waters.

All phenomena is illusion,
Neither attracted nor repelled,
Not making any sudden moves,
My habits will carry me through.

Sixth Chamber

These are the instructions for the Sixth Chamber of the First Hall of the Kingdom of Heaven.

As I experience the disintegration of my organic identity into the primal elements of consciousness in my passage through the eternal world, the tattered remnants of the world of matter surround me.

These apparitions of phenomena are my own evocations, emanating from my own primordial consciousness.

In the Sixth Chamber of the First Hall, the phantom reverberations of organic self-pity are consumed in thoughts of organic hunger, evoking illusions of the phenomenal world, and my attention is caught up in this distraction.

I remember the thoughts of organic hunger in my passage through the phenomenal world and, passing once again into the endless emptiness of the Void, these thoughts and images swirl upward in my consciousness. Not swept away by them into the magnetic force of sudden rebirth, I invoke the presence of the guardian of the Sixth Chamber of the First Hall of Heaven, the angel Anafiel, whose crown branches out to cover the whole of Heaven in a mantle of glory and majesty, who is a chief of celestial maintainers, keeper of the Keys of Heaven, who bore Enoch who was to become the angel Metatron to the Citadel of Heaven; the angel Anafiel I invoke.

Brilliant red radiation emanates from his heart, penetrating and dissolving all reverberations of organic hunger. At the same time, the phantom after-images of the phenomenal world, bathed in soft, smoky yellow light, seem to offer refuge from the cleansing radiation.

Not becoming engulfed in the seductive magnetic force of rebirth, I bathe in cleansing radiation, the brilliant red light dissolving all reverberations of the organic mind.

Wandering in the phantom images of the organic world, may my non-phenomenal self be cleansed by the brilliant radiation of the angel Anafiel; may inexorable reality be my guide.

May I remain impartial to phenomena, free from organic thoughts, not expelled in sudden rebirth.

May the blessed angel Anafiel be my protector. May he bring me safely through the Sixth Chamber of the First Hall which is his domain. May he help me to remember my non-phenomenal self.

Involved with thoughts of passionate possession,
Liberated from illusion of phenomena,
Separating into primal form,
Phenomena of senses.

Opening before me paths of endless passion,
Nothing there but misery and pain,
Serene and calm I wait in stillness and in silence,
Bathed in cleansing radiation.

Brilliant in the light of inner vision,
I see myself seductive and compelling,
Searching endlessly for satisfaction,
Always wanting more.

Penetrating radiation,
Red explosion from his heart to mine,
Another light, soft yellow, near the first,
Seems to offer refuge to my soul.

Melting in vibrating fusion,
Dissolving my resistance,
I lose the force of my reactions,
Not attracted to the yellow light.

Wandering alone among the hungry souls,
Bathed in cleansing radiation,
Surrendering myself
In endless crystal waters.

All phenomena is illusion,
Neither attracted nor repelled,
Not making any sudden moves,
My habits will carry me through.

Seventh Chamber

These are the instructions for the Seventh Chamber of the First Hall of the Kingdom of Heaven.

As I experience the disintegration of my organic identity into the primal elements of consciousness in my passage through the eternal world, the tattered remnants of the world of matter surround me.

These apparitions of phenomena are my own evocations, emanating from my own primordial consciousness.

In the Seventh Chamber of the First Hall, the phantom reverberations of organic hunger are consumed in thoughts of organic compulsions, evoking illusions of the phenomenal world, and my attention is caught up in this distraction.

I remember the thoughts of organic compulsions in my passage through the phenomenal world and, passing once again into the endless emptiness of the Void, these thoughts and images swirl upward in my consciousness. Not swept away by them into the magnetic force of sudden rebirth, I invoke the presence of the guardian of the Seventh Chamber of the First Hall of Heaven, the angel Hadriel, angel of self-punishment and remorse, who probes the soul and cleanses it of the dust of the phenomenal world, who spoke to Adam secrets unknown even to the angels; the angel Hadriel I invoke.

Brilliant orange radiation emanates from his heart, penetrating and dissolving all reverberations of organic compulsions. At the same time, the phantom after-images of the phenomenal world, bathed in soft, smoky violet light, seem to offer refuge from the cleansing radiation.

Not becoming engulfed in the seductive magnetic force of rebirth, I bathe in cleansing radiation, the brilliant orange light dissolving all reverberations of the organic mind.

Wandering in the phantom images of the organic world, may my non-phenomenal self be cleansed by the brilliant radiation of the angel Hadriel; may inexorable reality be my guide.

May I remain impartial to phenomena, free from organic thoughts, not expelled in sudden rebirth.

May the blessed angel Hadriel be my protector. May he bring me safely through the Seventh Chamber of the First Hall which is his domain. May he help me to remember my non-phenomenal self.

Involved with thoughts of my compulsive actions,
Swirling in a hurricane of force,
Separating into primal elements,
Phenomena of consciousness.

Opening before me paths of inattention,
Nothing there but misery and pain,
Serene and calm I wait in stillness and in silence,
Bathed in cleansing radiation.

Brilliant in the light of inner vision,
I see myself so comfortably familiar,
Master of all space and time,
Manifesting all phenomena.

Penetrating radiation,
Orange explosion from his heart to mine,
Another light, soft violet, near the first,
Seems to offer refuge to my soul.

Melting in vibrating fusion,
Dissolving my resistance,
I lose the force of my reactions,
Not attracted to the violet light.

Wandering alone in worlds of habit,
Bathed in cleansing radiation,
Surrendering myself
In endless crystal waters.

All phenomena is illusion,
Neither attracted nor repelled,
Not making any sudden moves,
My habits will carry me through.

Second Hall

In the Second Hall, the face of the lover is inflamed, burning and impetuous, ready to throw itself into the abyss of love without regret, as a landed fish struggles toward the water.

In the Second Hall, love is fire and reason goes up in smoke; when love appears, reason is obliterated. The reason of the mind cannot survive the folly of love. Love provides the special vision which makes visible the atoms of the non-phenomenal world.

As I make a passage through the Second Hall, I grow within myself a thousand hearts, that I may sacrifice one of them every moment.

Eighth Chamber

These are the instructions for the First Chamber of the Second Hall of the Kingdom of Heaven.

As I experience the disintegration of my organic identity into the primal elements of consciousness in my passage through the eternal world, the tattered remnants of the world of matter surround me.

These apparitions of phenomena are my own evocations, emanating from my own primordial consciousness.

In the First Chamber of the Second Hall, the phantom reverberations of organic compulsions are consumed in emotions of the organic mind, evoking illusions of the phenomenal world, and my attention is caught up in this distraction.

I remember the emotions of the organic mind in my passage through the phenomenal world and, passing once again into the endless emptiness of the Void, these emotions swirl upward in my consciousness. Not swept away by them into the magnetic force of sudden rebirth, I invoke the presence of the guardian of the First Chamber of the Second Hall of Heaven, the angel Tagriel, a chief of the angelic guardians of the Second Hall of Heaven and one of the twenty-eight rulers of the Lunar Chambers of Heaven, who takes the form of inanimate objects; the angel Tagriel I invoke.

Brilliant violet radiation emanates from his heart, penetrating and dissolving all reverberations of the organic mind. At the same time, the phantom after-images of the phenomenal world, bathed in soft, smoky orange light, seem to offer refuge from the cleansing radiation.

Not becoming engulfed in the seductive magnetic force of rebirth, I bathe in cleansing radiation, the brilliant violet light dissolving all reverberations of the organic mind.

Wandering in the phantom images of the organic world, may my non-phenomenal self be cleansed by the brilliant radiation of the angel Tagriel; may inexorable reality be my guide.

May I remain impartial to phenomena, free from organic emotions, not expelled in sudden rebirth.

May the blessed angel Tagriel be my protector. May he bring me safely through the First Chamber of the Second Hall which is his domain. May he help me to remember my non-phenomenal self.

Involved with emotions of solid form,
Swirling in a hurricane of force,
Separating into primal elements,
Phenomena of motion.

Opening before me paths of flesh and blood,
Nothing there but misery and pain,
Serene and calm I wait in stillness and in silence,
Bathed in cleansing radiation.

Brilliant in the light of inner vision,
I see my ego struggling for breath,
Clinging tightly to the remnants of organic life,
Terrified to die.

Penetrating radiation,
Violet explosion from his heart to mine,
Another light, soft orange, near the first,
Seems to offer refuge to my soul.

Melting in vibrating fusion,
Dissolving my resistance,
I lose the force of my reactions,
Not attracted to the orange light.

Wandering alone, maintaining feelings of body symptoms,
Bathed in cleansing radiation,
Surrendering myself
In endless crystal waters.

All phenomena is illusion,
Neither attracted nor repelled,
Not making any sudden moves,
My habits will carry me through.

Ninth Chamber

These are the instructions for the Second Chamber of the Second Hall of the Kingdom of Heaven.

As I experience the disintegration of my organic identity into the primal elements of consciousness in my passage through the eternal world, the tattered remnants of the world of matter surround me.

These apparitions of phenomena are my own evocations, emanating from my own primordial consciousness.

In the Second Chamber of the Second Hall, the phantom reverberations of the organic mind are consumed in emotions of my organic identity, evoking illusions of the phenomenal world, and my attention is caught up in this distraction.

I remember the emotions of my organic identity in my passage through the phenomenal world and, passing once again into the endless emptiness of the Void, these emotions swirl upward in my consciousness. Not swept away by them into the magnetic force of sudden rebirth, I invoke the presence of the guardian of the Second Chamber of the Second Hall of Heaven, the angel Sakhriel, who roams the Seven Halls of Heaven at his own will and who takes the form of a flame; the angel Sakhriel I invoke.

Brilliant blue radiation emanates from his heart, penetrating and dissolving all reverberations of my organic identity. At the same time, the phantom after-images of the phenomenal world, bathed in soft, smoky white light, seem to offer refuge from the cleansing radiation.

Not becoming engulfed in the seductive magnetic force of rebirth, I bathe in cleansing radiation, the brilliant blue light dissolving all reverberations of the organic mind.

Wandering in the phantom images of the organic world, may my non-phenomenal self be cleansed by the brilliant radiation of the angel Sakhriel; may inexorable reality be my guide.

May I remain impartial to phenomena, free from organic emotions, not expelled in sudden rebirth.

May the blessed angel Sakhriel be my protector. May he bring me safely through the Second Chamber of the Second Hall which is his domain. May he help me to remember my non-phenomenal self.

Involved with emotions of my identity,
Swirling in a hurricane of force,
Separating into primal elements,
Phenomena of dimension.

Opening before me paths of time and space,
Nothing there but misery and pain,
Serene and calm I wait in stillness and in silence,
Bathed in cleansing radiation.

Brilliant in the light of inner vision,
I see myself controlling destiny,
Clinging to the content of the mind,
Frozen memory.

Penetrating radiation,
Blue explosion from his heart to mine,
Another light, soft white, near the first,
Seems to offer refuge to my soul.

Melting in vibrating fusion,
Dissolving my resistance,
I lose the force of my reactions,
Not attracted to the soft white light.

Wandering alone, maintaining feelings of ego,
Bathed in cleansing radiation,
Surrendering myself
In endless crystal waters.

All phenomena is illusion,
Neither attracted nor repelled,
Not making any sudden moves,
My habits will carry me through.

Tenth Chamber

These are the instructions for the Third Chamber of the Second Hall of the Kingdom of Heaven.

As I experience the disintegration of my organic identity into the primal elements of consciousness in my passage through the eternal world, the tattered remnants of the world of matter surround me.

These apparitions of phenomena are my own evocations, emanating from my own primordial consciousness.

In the Third Chamber of the Second Hall, the phantom reverberations of my organic identity are consumed in emotions of organic fear, evoking illusions of the phenomenal world, and my attention is caught up in this distraction.

I remember the emotions of organic fear in my passage through the phenomenal world and, passing once again into the endless emptiness of the Void, these emotions swirl upward in my consciousness. Not swept away by them into the magnetic force of sudden rebirth, I invoke the presence of the guardian of the Third Chamber of the Second Hall of Heaven, the angel Adririon, mighty angelic chief in whose hands are the forces of healing both in Heaven and Earth, who can be called by the progressive subtraction of the final letter in his name; the angel Adririon I invoke.

Brilliant white radiation emanates from his heart, penetrating and dissolving all reverberations of organic fear. At the same time, the phantom after-images of the phenomenal world, bathed in soft, smoky black light, seem to offer refuge from the cleansing radiation.

Not becoming engulfed in the seductive magnetic force of rebirth, I bathe in cleansing radiation, the brilliant white light dissolving all reverberations of the organic mind.

Wandering in the phantom images of the organic world, may my non-phenomenal self be cleansed by the brilliant radiation of the angel Adririon; may inexorable reality be my guide.

May I remain impartial to phenomena, free from organic emotions, not expelled in sudden rebirth.

May the blessed angel Adririon be my protector. May he bring me safely through the Third Chamber of the Second Hall which is his domain. May he help me to remember my non-phenomenal self.

Involved with emotions of anxious expectation,
Swelling upward from my hidden self,
Separating into primal form,
Illusion of phenomena.

Opening before me paths of fear and anger,
Nothing there but misery and pain,
Serene and calm I wait in stillness and in silence,
Bathed in cleansing radiation.

Brilliant in the light of inner vision,
I see myself wreathed in seething hate,
Offering no sympathy or help,
Tantalizingly superior.

Penetrating radiation,
White explosion from his heart to mine,
Another light, soft black, near the first,
Seems to offer refuge to my soul.

Melting in vibrating fusion,
Dissolving my resistance,
I lose the force of my reactions,
Not attracted to the light of smoky black.

Wandering alone in worlds of fear,
Bathed in cleansing radiation,
Surrendering myself
In endless crystal waters.

All phenomena is illusion,
Neither attracted nor repelled,
Not making any sudden moves,
My habits will carry me through.

Eleventh Chamber

These are the instructions for the Fourth Chamber of the Second Hall of the Kingdom of Heaven.

As I experience the disintegration of my organic identity into the primal elements of consciousness in my passage through the eternal world, the tattered remnants of the world of matter surround me.

These apparitions of phenomena are my own evocations, emanating from my own primordial consciousness.

In the Fourth Chamber of the Second Hall, the phantom reverberations of organic fear are consumed in emotions of organic jealousy, evoking illusions of the phenomenal world, and my attention is caught up in this distraction.

I remember the emotions of organic jealousy in my passage through the phenomenal world and, passing once again into the endless emptiness of the Void, these emotions swirl upward in my consciousness. Not swept away by them into the magnetic force of sudden rebirth, I invoke the presence of the guardian of the Fourth Chamber of the Second Hall of Heaven, the angel Ashruliel, who causes the invisible angels to dwell within the visible world of phenomena, and who is a great angelic prince of the laws of cosmic harmony; the angel Ashruliel I invoke.

Brilliant green radiation emanates from his heart, penetrating and dissolving all reverberations of organic jealousy. At the same time, the phantom after-images of the phenomenal world, bathed in soft, smoky red light, seem to offer refuge from the cleansing radiation.

Not becoming engulfed in the seductive magnetic force of rebirth, I bathe in cleansing radiation, the brilliant green light dissolving all reverberations of the organic mind.

Wandering in the phantom images of the organic world, may my non-phenomenal self be cleansed by the brilliant radiation of the angel Ashruliel; may inexorable reality be my guide.

May I remain impartial to phenomena, free from organic emotions, not expelled in sudden rebirth.

May the blessed angel Ashruliel be my protector. May he bring me safely through the Fourth Chamber of the Second Hall which is his domain. May he help me to remember my non-phenomenal self.

Involved with emotions of jealousy and competition,
Rising upward from my hidden self,
Separating into primal form,
Repulsively attractive.

Opening before me paths of lingering uncertainty,
Nothing there but misery and pain,
Serene and calm I wait in stillness and in silence,
Bathed in cleansing radiation.

Brilliant in the light of inner vision,
I see myself suspiciously distrustful,
Clinging to my every action,
Gnawing at my soul.

Penetrating radiation,
Green explosion from his heart to mine,
Another light, soft red, near the first,
Seems to offer refuge to my soul.

Melting in vibrating fusion,
Dissolving my resistance,
I lose the force of my reactions,
Not attracted to the soft red light.

Wandering alone in worlds of jealousy,
Bathed in cleansing radiation,
Surrendering myself
In endless crystal waters.

All phenomena is illusion,
Neither attracted nor repelled,
Not making any sudden moves,
My habits will carry me through.

Twelfth Chamber

These are the instructions for the Fifth Chamber of the Second Hall of the Kingdom of Heaven.

As I experience the disintegration of my organic identity into the primal elements of consciousness in my passage through the eternal world, the tattered remnants of the world of matter surround me.

These apparitions of phenomena are my own evocations, emanating from my own primordial consciousness.

In the Fifth Chamber of the Second Hall, the phantom reverberations of organic jealousy are consumed in emotions of organic self-pity, evoking illusions of the phenomenal world, and my attention is caught up in this distraction.

I remember the emotions of organic self-pity in my passage through the phenomenal world and, passing once again into the endless emptiness of the Void, these emotions swirl upward in my consciousness. Not swept away by them into the magnetic force of sudden rebirth, I invoke the presence of the guardian of the Fifth Chamber of the Second Hall of Heaven, the angel Sabriel, one of the seven great archangels, a chief of the Order of *Tarshishim*, who are called the brilliant angels, the only angel with the power to overcome the fallen angel Sphendonael, the demon of disease; the angel Sabriel I invoke.

Brilliant yellow radiation emanates from his heart, penetrating and dissolving all reverberations of organic self-pity. At the same time, the phantom after-images of the phenomenal world, bathed in soft, smoky blue light, seem to offer refuge from the cleansing radiation.

Not becoming engulfed in the seductive magnetic force of rebirth, I bathe in cleansing radiation, the brilliant yellow light dissolving all reverberations of the organic mind.

Wandering in the phantom images of the organic world, may my non-phenomenal self be cleansed by the brilliant radiation of the angel Sabriel; may inexorable reality be my guide.

May I remain impartial to phenomena, free from organic emotions, not expelled in sudden rebirth.

May the blessed angel Sabriel be my protector. May he bring me safely through the Fifth Chamber of the Second Hall which is his domain. May he help me to remember my non-phenomenal self.

Involved with emotions of vanity and arrogance,
Towering above myself in pride,
Separating into primal form,
Immovably secure.

Opening before me paths of isolation,
Nothing there but misery and pain,
Serene and calm I wait in stillness and in silence,
Bathed in cleansing radiation.

Brilliant in the light of inner vision,
I see myself inferior and foolish,
Holding tightly to the past and present,
Terrified to bend.

Penetrating radiation,
Yellow explosion from his heart to mine,
Another light, soft blue, near the first,
Seems to offer refuge to my soul.

Melting in vibrating fusion,
Dissolving my resistance,
I lose the force of my reactions,
Not attracted to the soft blue light.

Wandering alone in worlds of pride,
Bathed in cleansing radiation,
Surrendering myself
In endless crystal waters.

All phenomena is illusion,
Neither attracted nor repelled,
Not making any sudden moves,
My habits will carry me through.

Thirteenth Chamber

These are the instructions for the Sixth Chamber of the Second Hall of the Kingdom of Heaven.

As I experience the disintegration of my organic identity into the primal elements of consciousness in my passage through the eternal world, the tattered remnants of the world of matter surround me.

These apparitions of phenomena are my own evocations, emanating from my own primordial consciousness.

In the Sixth Chamber of the Second Hall, the phantom reverberations of organic self-pity are consumed in emotions of organic hunger, evoking illusions of the phenomenal world, and my attention is caught up in this distraction.

I remember the emotions of organic hunger in my passage through the phenomenal world and, passing once again into the endless emptiness of the Void, these emotions swirl upward in my consciousness. Not swept away by them into the magnetic force of sudden rebirth, I invoke the presence of the guardian of the Sixth Chamber of the Second Hall of Heaven, the angel Akatriel, one of the great crown princes of judgment, who is placed over all other angels and men, and is the angel of the Lord of Hosts, who was summoned with his hundred and twenty myriads of serving angels to subdue the fallen angel Samael, the prince of evil; the angel Akatriel I invoke.

Brilliant red radiation emanates from his heart, penetrating and dissolving all reverberations of organic hunger. At the same time, the phantom after-images of the phenomenal world, bathed in soft, smoky yellow light, seem to offer refuge from the cleansing radiation.

Not becoming engulfed in the seductive magnetic force of rebirth, I bathe in cleansing radiation, the brilliant red light dissolving all reverberations of the organic mind.

Wandering in the phantom images of the organic world, may my non-phenomenal self be cleansed by the brilliant radiation of the angel Akatriel; may inexorable reality be my guide.

May I remain impartial to phenomena, free from organic emotions, not expelled in sudden rebirth.

May the blessed angel Akatriel be my protector. May he bring me safely through the Sixth Chamber of the Second Hall which is his domain. May he help me to remember my non-phenomenal self.

Involved with emotions of passionate possession,
Liberated from illusion of phenomena,
Separating into primal form,
Phenomena of senses.

Opening before me paths of endless passion,
Nothing there but misery and pain,
Serene and calm I wait in stillness and in silence,
Bathed in cleansing radiation.

Brilliant in the light of inner vision,
I see myself seductive and compelling,
Searching endlessly for satisfaction,
Always wanting more.

Penetrating radiation,
Red explosion from his heart to mine,
Another light, soft yellow, near the first,
Seems to offer refuge to my soul.

Melting in vibrating fusion,
Dissolving my resistance,
I lose the force of my reactions,
Not attracted to the yellow light.

Wandering alone among the hungry souls,
Bathed in cleansing radiation,
Surrendering myself
In endless crystal waters.

All phenomena is illusion,
Neither attracted nor repelled,
Not making any sudden moves,
My habits will carry me through.

Fourteenth Chamber

These are the instructions for the Seventh Chamber of the Second Hall of the Kingdom of Heaven.

As I experience the disintegration of my organic identity into the primal elements of consciousness in my passage through the eternal world, the tattered remnants of the world of matter surround me.

These apparitions of phenomena are my own evocations, emanating from my own primordial consciousness.

In the Seventh Chamber of the Second Hall, the phantom reverberations of organic hunger are consumed in emotions of organic compulsions, evoking illusions of the phenomenal world, and my attention is caught up in this distraction.

I remember the emotions of organic compulsions in my passage through the phenomenal world and, passing once again into the endless emptiness of the Void, these emotions swirl upward in my consciousness. Not swept away by them into the magnetic force of sudden rebirth, I invoke the presence of the guardian of the Seventh Chamber of the Second Hall of Heaven, the angel Azbugah, one of the eight great angels of the throne of judgment, who holds a rank superior even to that of Metatron, whose duty it is to clothe with righteousness those who arrive in Heaven and are deemed worthy, and who is invoked for the healing of pain and suffering which linger in reverberation from the organic world; the angel Azbugah I invoke.

Brilliant orange radiation emanates from his heart, penetrating and dissolving all reverberations of organic compulsions. At the same time, the phantom after-images of the phenomenal world, bathed in soft, smoky violet light, seem to offer refuge from the cleansing radiation.

Not becoming engulfed in the seductive magnetic force of rebirth, I bathe in cleansing radiation, the brilliant orange light dissolving all reverberations of the organic mind.

Wandering in the phantom images of the organic world, may my non-phenomenal self be cleansed by the brilliant radiation of the angel Azbugah; may inexorable reality be my guide.

May I remain impartial to phenomena, free from organic emotions, not expelled in sudden rebirth.

May the blessed angel Azbugah be my protector. May he bring me safely through the Seventh Chamber of the Second Hall which is his domain. May he help me to remember my non-phenomenal self.

Involved with emotions of my compulsive actions,
Swirling in a hurricane of force,
Separating into primal elements,
Phenomena of consciousness.

Opening before me paths of inattention,
Nothing there but misery and pain,
Serene and calm I wait in stillness and in silence,
Bathed in cleansing radiation.

Brilliant in the light of inner vision,
I see myself so comfortably familiar,
Master of all space and time,
Manifesting all phenomena.

Penetrating radiation,
Orange explosion from his heart to mine,
Another light, soft violet, near the first,
Seems to offer refuge to my soul.

Melting in vibrating fusion,
Dissolving my resistance,
I lose the force of my reactions,
Not attracted to the violet light.

Wandering alone in worlds of habit,
Bathed in cleansing radiation,
Surrendering myself
In endless crystal waters.

All phenomena is illusion,
Neither attracted nor repelled,
Not making any sudden moves,
My habits will carry me through.

Third Hall

The Third Hall has neither beginning nor end; the distance to be traveled is beyond imagination. Only against this backdrop of endless emptiness do weakness, sleep and hallucination reveal themselves to my vision.

If a gnat beat its wings with all its might, it could not equal the power of the wind. From the vision of the thousand-faceted diamond, the fragmented infinite polyhedron, I suddenly behold the perfect sphere; from the vision of the many I penetrate to the vision of the One; the patchwork quilt which is the King Himself — many-hued, clothed in endless dazzling splendor, robed in myriads of secrets; from the vision of the ocean I penetrate to the vision of the single drop of water within which the play of light dances endlessly, fascinating and compelling, infinite hypnotic forms.

Fifteenth Chamber

These are the instructions for the First Chamber of the Third Hall of the Kingdom of Heaven.

As I experience the disintegration of my organic identity into the primal elements of consciousness in my passage through the eternal world, the tattered remnants of the world of matter surround me.

These apparitions of phenomena are my own evocations, emanating from my own primordial consciousness.

In the First Chamber of the Third Hall, the phantom reverberations of organic compulsions are consumed in apprehensions about the organic mind, evoking illusions of the phenomenal world, and my attention is caught up in this distraction.

I remember my apprehensions about the organic mind in my passage through the phenomenal world and, passing once again into the endless emptiness of the Void, these apprehensions swirl upward in my consciousness. Not swept away by them into the magnetic force of sudden rebirth, I invoke the presence of the guardian of the First Chamber of the Third Hall of Heaven, the angel Barakiel, who is called the lightning of God and who is one of the seven great archangels, one of the four ruling Seraphim, the angel of confession and one of the chief angels of the angelic choruses which are charged with the invocation of the phenomenal world through the incantation of sound in the form of prayer and sacred canticles; the angel Barakiel I invoke.

Brilliant violet radiation emanates from his heart, penetrating and dissolving all reverberations of the organic mind. At the same time, the phantom after-images of the phenomenal world, bathed in soft, smoky orange light, seem to offer refuge from the cleansing radiation.

Not becoming engulfed in the seductive magnetic force of rebirth, I bathe in cleansing radiation, the brilliant violet light dissolving all reverberations of the organic mind.

Wandering in the phantom images of the organic world, may my non-phenomenal self be cleansed by the brilliant radiation of the angel Barakiel; may inexorable reality be my guide.

May I remain impartial to phenomena, free from organic apprehensions, not expelled in sudden rebirth.

May the blessed angel Barakiel be my protector. May he bring me safely through the First Chamber of the Third Hall which is his domain. May he help me to remember my non-phenomenal self.

Involved with apprehensions about solid form,
Swirling in a hurricane of force,
Separating into primal elements,
Phenomena of motion.

Opening before me paths of flesh and blood,
Nothing there but misery and pain,
Serene and calm I wait in stillness and in silence,
Bathed in cleansing radiation.

Brilliant in the light of inner vision,
I see my ego struggling for breath,
Clinging tightly to the remnants of organic life,
Terrified to die.

Penetrating radiation,
Violet explosion from his heart to mine,
Another light, soft orange, near the first,
Seems to offer refuge to my soul.

Melting in vibrating fusion,
Dissolving my resistance,
I lose the force of my reactions,
Not attracted to the orange light.

Wandering alone, maintaining apprehensions about
    body symptoms,
Bathed in cleansing radiation,
Surrendering myself
In endless crystal waters.

All phenomena is illusion,
Neither attracted nor repelled,
Not making any sudden moves,
My habits will carry me through.

Sixteenth Chamber

These are the instructions for the Second Chamber of the Third Hall of the Kingdom of Heaven.

As I experience the disintegration of my organic identity into the primal elements of consciousness in my passage through the eternal world, the tattered remnants of the world of matter surround me.

These apparitions of phenomena are my own evocations, emanating from my own primordial consciousness.

In the Second Chamber of the Third Hall, the phantom reverberations of the organic mind are consumed in apprehensions about my organic identity, evoking illusions of the phenomenal world, and my attention is caught up in this distraction.

I remember my apprehensions about my organic identity in my passage through the phenomenal world and, passing once again into the endless emptiness of the Void, these apprehensions swirl upward in my consciousness. Not swept away by them into the magnetic force of sudden rebirth, I invoke the presence of the guardian of the Second Chamber of the Third Hall of Heaven, the angel Kemuel, he who is able to see God without averting his eyes, a chief of the Order of Powers, one of the ten wardens of the non-phenomenal world, who is the per-sonification of divine inexorable justice, who wrestled with Jacob and who appeared to Jesus in the Garden of Gethsemane, a chief of the Order of Dominations, the great Archon who stands at the gates of Heaven as the mediator between the prayers of men and the prayers of angels; the angel Kemuel I invoke.

Brilliant blue radiation emanates from his heart, penetrating and dissolving all reverberations of my organic identity. At the same time, the phantom after-images of the phenomenal world, bathed in soft, smoky white light, seem to offer refuge from the cleansing radiation.

Not becoming engulfed in the seductive magnetic force of rebirth, I bathe in cleansing radiation, the brilliant blue light dissolving all reverberations of the organic mind.

Wandering in the phantom images of the organic world, may my non-phenomenal self be cleansed by the brilliant radiation of the angel Kemuel; may inexorable reality be my guide.

May I remain impartial to phenomena, free from organic apprehensions, not expelled in sudden rebirth.

May the blessed angel Kemuel be my protector. May he bring me safely through the Second Chamber of the Third Hall which is his domain. May he help me to remember my non-phenomenal self.

Involved with apprehensions about my identity,
Swirling in a hurricane of force,
Separating into primal elements,
Phenomena of dimension.

Opening before me paths of time and space,
Nothing there but misery and pain,
Serene and calm I wait in stillness and in silence,
Bathed in cleansing radiation.

Brilliant in the light of inner vision,
I see myself controlling destiny,
Clinging to the content of the mind,
Frozen memory.

Penetrating radiation,
Blue explosion from his heart to mine,
Another light, soft white, near the first,
Seems to offer refuge to my soul.

Melting in vibrating fusion,
Dissolving my resistance,
I lose the force of my reactions,
Not attracted to the soft white light.

Wandering alone, maintaining apprehensions about ego,
Bathed in cleansing radiation,
Surrendering myself
In endless crystal waters.

All phenomena is illusion,
Neither attracted nor repelled,
Not making any sudden moves,
My habits will carry me through.

Seventeenth Chamber

These are the instructions for the Third Chamber of the Third Hall of the Kingdom of Heaven.

As I experience the disintegration of my organic identity into the primal elements of consciousness in my passage through the eternal world, the tattered remnants of the world of matter surround me.

These apparitions of phenomena are my own evocations, emanating from my own primordial consciousness.

In the Third Chamber of the Third Hall, the phantom reverberations of my organic identity are consumed in apprehensions about organic fear, evoking illusions of the phenomenal world, and my attention is caught up in this distraction.

I remember my apprehensions about organic fear in my passage through the phenomenal world and, passing once again into the endless emptiness of the Void, these apprehensions swirl upward in my consciousness. Not swept away by them into the magnetic force of sudden rebirth, I invoke the presence of the guardian of the Third Chamber of the Third Hall of Heaven, the angel Chayyiel, a ruling prince of the *Hayyoth*, before whom all children of Heaven tremble, who can swallow the world in one moment, who flogs the ministering angels who fail to chant the sacred canticles and who surrounds the Throne of God with fire and has dominion over all wild animals; a chief of the Order of Dominations, who, when he speaks, fills the air with flames; the angel Chayyiel I invoke.

Brilliant white radiation emanates from his heart, penetrating and dissolving all reverberations of organic fear. At the same time, the phantom after-images of the phenomenal world, bathed in soft, smoky black light, seem to offer refuge from the cleansing radiation.

Not becoming engulfed in the seductive magnetic force of rebirth, I bathe in cleansing radiation, the brilliant white light dissolving all reverberations of the organic mind.

Wandering in the phantom images of the organic world, may my non-phenomenal self be cleansed by the brilliant radiation of the angel Chayyiel; may inexorable reality be my guide.

May I remain impartial to phenomena, free from organic apprehensions, not expelled in sudden rebirth.

May the blessed angel Chayyiel be my protector. May he bring me safely through the Third Chamber of the Third Hall which is his domain. May he help me to remember my non-phenomenal self.

Involved with anxious expectation,
Swelling upward from my hidden self,
Separating into primal form,
Illusion of phenomena.

Opening before me paths of fear and anger,
Nothing there but misery and pain,
Serene and calm I wait in stillness and in silence,
Bathed in cleansing radiation.

Brilliant in the light of inner vision,
I see myself wreathed in seething hate,
Offering no sympathy or help,
Tantalizingly superior.

Penetrating radiation,
White explosion from his heart to mine,
Another light, soft black, near the first,
Seems to offer refuge to my soul.

Melting in vibrating fusion,
Dissolving my resistance,
I lose the force of my reactions,
Not attracted to the light of smoky black.

Wandering alone in worlds of fear,
Bathed in cleansing radiation,
Surrendering myself
In endless crystal waters.

All phenomena is illusion,
Neither attracted nor repelled,
Not making any sudden moves,
My habits will carry me through.

Eighteenth Chamber

These are the instructions for the Fourth Chamber of the Third Hall of the Kingdom of Heaven.

As I experience the disintegration of my organic identity into the primal elements of consciousness in my passage through the eternal world, the tattered remnants of the world of matter surround me.

These apparitions of phenomena are my own evocations, emanating from my own primordial consciousness.

In the Fourth Chamber of the Third Hall, the phantom reverberations of organic fear are consumed in apprehensions about organic jealousy, evoking illusions of the phenomenal world, and my attention is caught up in this distraction.

I remember my apprehensions about organic jealousy in my passage through the phenomenal world and, passing once again into the endless emptiness of the Void, these apprehensions swirl upward in my consciousness. Not swept away by them into the magnetic force of sudden rebirth, I invoke the presence of the guardian of the Fourth Chamber of the Third Hall of Heaven, the angel Galgaliel, chief angel of the Solar Absolute, governor of the wheel of fire, a chief of the Order of *Galgalim;* the angel Galgaliel I invoke.

Brilliant green radiation emanates from his heart, penetrating and dissolving all reverberations of organic jealousy. At the same time, the phantom after-images of the phenomenal world, bathed in soft, smoky red light, seem to offer refuge from the cleansing radiation.

Not becoming engulfed in the seductive magnetic force of rebirth, I bathe in cleansing radiation, the brilliant green light dissolving all reverberations of the organic mind.

Wandering in the phantom images of the organic world, may my non-phenomenal self be cleansed by the brilliant radiation of the angel Galgaliel; may inexorable reality be my guide.

May I remain impartial to phenomena, free from organic apprehensions, not expelled in sudden rebirth.

May the blessed angel Galgaliel be my protector. May he bring me safely through the Fourth Chamber of the Third Hall which is his domain. May he help me to remember my non-phenomenal self.

Involved with apprehensions about jealousy and competition,
Rising upward from my hidden self,
Separating into primal form,
Repulsively attractive.

Opening before me paths of lingering uncertainty,
Nothing there but misery and pain,
Serene and calm I wait in stillness and in silence,
Bathed in cleansing radiation.

Brilliant in the light of inner vision,
I see myself suspiciously distrustful,
Clinging to my every action,
Gnawing at my soul.

Penetrating radiation,
Green explosion from his heart to mine,
Another light, soft red, near the first,
Seems to offer refuge to my soul.

Melting in vibrating fusion,
Dissolving my resistance,
I lose the force of my reactions,
Not attracted to the soft red light.

Wandering alone in worlds of jealousy,
Bathed in cleansing radiation,
Surrendering myself
In endless crystal waters.

All phenomena is illusion,
Neither attracted nor repelled,
Not making any sudden moves,
My habits will carry me through.

Nineteenth Chamber

These are the instructions for the Fifth Chamber of the Third Hall of the Kingdom of Heaven.

As I experience the disintegration of my organic identity into the primal elements of consciousness in my passage through the eternal world, the tattered remnants of the world of matter surround me.

These apparitions of phenomena are my own evocations, emanating from my own primordial consciousness.

In the Fifth Chamber of the Third Hall, the phantom reverberations of organic jealousy are consumed in apprehensions about organic self-pity, evoking illusions of the phenomenal world, and my attention is caught up in this distraction.

I remember my apprehensions about organic self-pity in my passage through the phenomenal world and, passing once again into the endless emptiness of the Void, these apprehensions swirl upward in my consciousness. Not swept away by them into the magnetic force of sudden rebirth, I invoke the presence of the guardian of the Fifth Chamber of the Third Hall of Heaven, the angel Aniel, who is called the Grace of God, angel of the month December, a chief of the Order of Principalities and Virtues, and governor of the signs of Capricorn and Venus, who stands among the seven great archangels and the ten Holy *Sephiroth;* the angel Aniel I invoke.

Brilliant yellow radiation emanates from his heart, penetrating and dissolving all reverberations of organic self-pity. At the same time, the phantom after-images of the phenomenal world, bathed in soft, smoky blue light, seem to offer refuge from the cleansing radiation.

Not becoming engulfed in the seductive magnetic force of rebirth, I bathe in cleansing radiation, the brilliant yellow light dissolving all reverberations of the organic mind.

Wandering in the phantom images of the organic world, may my non-phenomenal self be cleansed by the brilliant radiation of the angel Aniel; may inexorable reality be my guide.

May I remain impartial to phenomena, free from organic apprehensions, not expelled in sudden rebirth.

May the blessed angel Aniel be my protector. May he bring me safely through the Fifth Chamber of the Third Hall which is his domain. May he help me to remember my non-phenomenal self.

Involved with apprehensions about vanity and arrogance,
Towering above myself in pride,
Separating into primal form,
Immovably secure.

Opening before me paths of isolation,
Nothing there but misery and pain,
Serene and calm I wait in stillness and in silence,
Bathed in cleansing radiation.

Brilliant in the light of inner vision,
I see myself inferior and foolish,
Holding tightly to the past and present,
Terrified to bend.

Penetrating radiation,
Yellow explosion from his heart to mine,
Another light, soft blue, near the first,
Seems to offer refuge to my soul.

Melting in vibrating fusion,
Dissolving my resistance,
I lose the force of my reactions,
Not attracted to the soft blue light.

Wandering alone in worlds of pride,
Bathed in cleansing radiation,
Surrendering myself
In endless crystal waters.

All phenomena is illusion,
Neither attracted nor repelled,
Not making any sudden moves,
My habits will carry me through.

Twentieth Chamber

These are the instructions for the Sixth Chamber of the Third Hall of the Kingdom of Heaven.

As I experience the disintegration of my organic identity into the primal elements of consciousness in my passage through the eternal world, the tattered remnants of the world of matter surround me.

These apparitions of phenomena are my own evocations, emanating from my own primordial consciousness.

In the Sixth Chamber of the Third Hall, the phantom reverberations of organic self-pity are consumed in apprehensions about organic hunger, evoking illusions of the phenomenal world, and my attention is caught up in this distraction.

I remember my apprehensions about organic hunger in my passage through the phenomenal world and, passing once again into the endless emptiness of the Void, these apprehensions swirl upward in my consciousness. Not swept away by them into the magnetic force of sudden rebirth, I invoke the presence of the guardian of the Sixth Chamber of the Third Hall of Heaven, the angel Iofiel, who is called the beauty of God, companion angel of Metatron, a prince of the Holy Law, one of the seven great archangels, a ruler of Saturn and the invoked presence of the planet Jupiter, who drove Adam from the Garden of Eden, a ruler of the Order of Cherubim, a chief of the Order of Thrones, who taught Moses the mystery of the Kabala, who teaches to men all the languages of the phenomenal world; the angel Iofiel I invoke.

Brilliant red radiation emanates from his heart, penetrating and dissolving all reverberations of organic hunger. At the same time, the phantom after-images of the phenomenal world, bathed in soft, smoky yellow light, seem to offer refuge from the cleansing radiation.

Not becoming engulfed in the seductive magnetic force of rebirth, I bathe in cleansing radiation, the brilliant red light dissolving all reverberations of the organic mind.

Wandering in the phantom images of the organic world, may my non-phenomenal self be cleansed by the brilliant radiation of the angel Iofiel; may inexorable reality be my guide.

May I remain impartial to phenomena, free from organic apprehensions, not expelled in sudden rebirth.

May the blessed angel Iofiel be my protector. May he bring me safely through the Sixth Chamber of the Third Hall which is his domain. May he help me to remember my non-phenomenal self.

Involved with apprehensions about passionate possession,
Liberated from illusion of phenomena,
Separating into primal form,
Phenomena of senses.

Opening before me paths of endless passion,
Nothing there but misery and pain,
Serene and calm I wait in stillness and in silence,
Bathed in cleansing radiation.

Brilliant in the light of inner vision,
I see myself seductive and compelling,
Searching endlessly for satisfaction,
Always wanting more.

Penetrating radiation,
Red explosion from his heart to mine,
Another light, soft yellow, near the first,
Seems to offer refuge to my soul.

Melting in vibrating fusion,
Dissolving my resistance,
I lose the force of my reactions,
Not attracted to the yellow light.

Wandering alone among the hungry souls,
Bathed in cleansing radiation,
Surrendering myself
In endless crystal waters.

All phenomena is illusion,
Neither attracted nor repelled,
Not making any sudden moves,
My habits will carry me through.

Twenty-First Chamber

These are the instructions for the Seventh Chamber of the Third Hall of the Kingdom of Heaven.

As I experience the disintegration of my organic identity into the primal elements of consciousness in my passage through the eternal world, the tattered remnants of the world of matter surround me.

These apparitions of phenomena are my own evocations, emanating from my own primordial consciousness.

In the Seventh Chamber of the Third Hall, the phantom reverberations of organic hunger are consumed in apprehensions about organic compulsions, evoking illusions of the phenomenal world, and my attention is caught up in this distraction.

I remember my apprehensions about organic compulsions in my passage through the phenomenal world and, passing once again into the endless emptiness of the Void, these apprehensions swirl upward in my consciousness. Not swept away by them into the magnetic force of sudden rebirth, I invoke the presence of the guardian of the Seventh Chamber of the Third Hall of Heaven, the angel Jehoel, mediator of the Ineffable Name, one of the Princes of the Presence of God, the angel who holds the Leviathan in check, the heavenly choirmaster who accompanied Abraham to Heaven and revealed to him the whole course of human history; the angel Jehoel I invoke.

Brilliant orange radiation emanates from his heart, penetrating and dissolving all reverberations of organic compulsions. At the same time, the phantom after-images of the phenomenal world, bathed in soft, smoky violet light, seem to offer refuge from the cleansing radiation.

Not becoming engulfed in the seductive magnetic force of rebirth, I bathe in cleansing radiation, the brilliant orange light dissolving all reverberations of the organic mind.

Wandering in the phantom images of the organic world, may my non-phenomenal self be cleansed by the brilliant radiation of the angel Jehoel; may inexorable reality be my guide.

May I remain impartial to phenomena, free from organic apprehensions, not expelled in sudden rebirth.

May the blessed angel Jehoel be my protector. May he bring me safely through the Seventh Chamber of the Third Hall which is his domain. May he help me to remember my non-phenomenal self.

Involved with apprehensions about my compulsive actions,
Swirling in a hurricane of force,
Separating into primal elements,
Phenomena of consciousness.

Opening before me paths of inattention,
Nothing there but misery and pain,
Serene and calm I wait in stillness and in silence,
Bathed in cleansing radiation.

Brilliant in the light of inner vision,
I see myself so comfortably familiar,
Master of all space and time,
Manifesting all phenomena.

Penetrating radiation,
Orange explosion from his heart to mine,
Another light, soft violet, near the first,
Seems to offer refuge to my soul.

Melting in vibrating fusion,
Dissolving my resistance,
I lose the force of my reactions,
Not attracted to the violet light.

Wandering alone in worlds of habit,
Bathed in cleansing radiation,
Surrendering myself
In endless crystal waters.

All phenomena is illusion,
Neither attracted nor repelled,
Not making any sudden moves,
My habits will carry me through.

Fourth Hall

In the Fourth Hall there is no desire to possess objects, no impulse to discover new things. A cold wind blows so violently that, in the blink of an eye, an immense space is devastated.

The oceans are a mere pool, the planets bits of mud, the sun just a dim spark in an endless sea of fire, the phenomenal world an empty corpse.

Just so that the First Adam might descend to the phenomenal world, hosts of angels were consumed; that Noah might build the ark, millions of creatures perished in the flood; that Jesus might possess the Secret of the Christ, millions took the Christian vows; that Mohammed might ascend to Heaven for a single night, millions of souls were pillaged.

In the Fourth Hall, nothing of the phenomenal world, neither ancient nor modern, has meaning. If a whole world burned, it would be only the dream of an angel. If Heaven and Earth were vaporized into atoms it would mean no more than a leaf falling from a tree; if the universe were annihilated in a single instant, leaving no trace of men or angels, it would be no more than the mystery of a single drop of water from which all the brilliant, sparkling, dazzling shattered fragments of light called the phenomenal world were formed.

Twenty-Second Chamber

These are the instructions for the First Chamber of the Fourth Hall of the Kingdom of Heaven.

As I experience the disintegration of my organic identity into the primal elements of consciousness in my passage through the eternal world, the tattered remnants of the world of matter surround me.

These apparitions of phenomena are my own evocations, emanating from my own primordial consciousness.

In the First Chamber of the Fourth Hall, the phantom reverberations of organic compulsions are consumed in the significance of the organic mind, evoking illusions of the phenomenal world, and my attention is caught up in this distraction.

I remember the significance of the organic mind in my passage through the phenomenal world and, passing once again into the endless emptiness of the Void, this significance swirls upward in my consciousness. Not swept away by it into the magnetic force of sudden rebirth, I invoke the presence of the guardian of the First Chamber of the Fourth Hall of Heaven, the angel Phanuel, called the Face of God, archangel of remorse, one of the four angels of the Presence of the Absolute, who knows all the evil which men of Earth have committed and who acts as shepherd to the spirits of those who are voyagers in the world of spirit as they pass from the world of phenomena; the angel Phanuel I invoke.

Brilliant violet radiation emanates from his heart, penetrating and dissolving all reverberations of the organic mind. At the same time, the phantom after-images of the phenomenal world, bathed in soft, smoky orange light, seem to offer refuge from the cleansing radiation.

Not becoming engulfed in the seductive magnetic force of rebirth, I bathe in cleansing radiation, the brilliant violet light dissolving all reverberations of the organic mind.

Wandering in the phantom images of the organic world, may my non-phenomenal self be cleansed by the brilliant radiation of the angel Phanuel; may inexorable reality be my guide.

May I remain impartial to phenomena, free from organic significance, not expelled in sudden rebirth.

May the blessed angel Phanuel be my protector. May he bring me safely through the First Chamber of the Fourth Hall which is his domain. May he help me to remember my non-phenomenal self.

Involved with significance of solid form,
Swirling in a hurricane of force,
Separating into primal elements,
Phenomena of motion.

Opening before me paths of flesh and blood,
Nothing there but misery and pain,
Serene and calm I wait in stillness and in silence,
Bathed in cleansing radiation.

Brilliant in the light of inner vision,
I see my ego struggling for breath,
Clinging tightly to the remnants of organic life,
Terrified to die.

Penetrating radiation,
Violet explosion from his heart to mine,
Another light, soft orange, near the first,
Seems to offer refuge to my soul.

Melting in vibrating fusion,
Dissolving my resistance,
I lose the force of my reactions,
Not attracted to the orange light.

Wandering alone, maintaining significance of body symptoms,
Bathed in cleansing radiation,
Surrendering myself
In endless crystal waters.

All phenomena is illusion,
Neither attracted nor repelled,
Not making any sudden moves,
My habits will carry me through.

Twenty-Third Chamber

These are the instructions for the Second Chamber of the Fourth Hall of the Kingdom of Heaven.

As I experience the disintegration of my organic identity into the primal elements of consciousness in my passage through the eternal world, the tattered remnants of the world of matter surround me.

These apparitions of phenomena are my own evocations, emanating from my own primordial consciousness.

In the Second Chamber of the Fourth Hall, the phantom reverberations of the organic mind are consumed in the significance of my organic identity, evoking illusions of the phenomenal world, and my attention is caught up in this distraction.

I remember the significance of my organic identity in my passage through the phenomenal world and, passing once again into the endless emptiness of the Void, this significance swirls upward in my consciousness. Not swept away by it into the magnetic force of sudden rebirth, I invoke the presence of the guardian of the Second Chamber of the Fourth Hall of Heaven, the angel Ragiel, who is called Friend of God, one of the great archangels who brings other angels to judgment, who spoke with Michael concerning the fallen angels and was the shepherd of the thrice-great Hermes; the angel Ragiel I invoke.

Brilliant blue radiation emanates from his heart, penetrating and dissolving all reverberations of my organic identity. At the same time, the phantom after-images of the phenomenal world, bathed in soft, smoky white light, seem to offer refuge from the cleansing radiation.

Not becoming engulfed in the seductive magnetic force of rebirth, I bathe in cleansing radiation, the brilliant blue light dissolving all reverberations of the organic mind.

Wandering in the phantom images of the organic world, may my non-phenomenal self be cleansed by the brilliant radiation of the angel Ragiel; may inexorable reality be my guide.

May I remain impartial to phenomena, free from organic significance, not expelled in sudden rebirth.

May the blessed angel Ragiel be my protector. May he bring me safely through the Second Chamber of the Fourth Hall which is his domain. May he help me to remember my non-phenomenal self.

Involved with significance of my identity,
Swirling in a hurricane of force,
Separating into primal elements,
Phenomena of dimension.

Opening before me paths of time and space,
Nothing there but misery and pain,
Serene and calm I wait in stillness and in silence,
Bathed in cleansing radiation.

Brilliant in the light of inner vision,
I see myself controlling destiny,
Clinging to the content of the mind,
Frozen memory.

Penetrating radiation,
Blue explosion from his heart to mine,
Another light, soft white, near the first,
Seems to offer refuge to my soul.

Melting in vibrating fusion,
Dissolving my resistance,
I lose the force of my reactions,
Not attracted to the soft white light.

Wandering alone, maintaining significance of ego,
Bathed in cleansing radiation,
Surrendering myself
In endless crystal waters.

All phenomena is illusion,
Neither attracted nor repelled,
Not making any sudden moves,
My habits will carry me through.

Twenty-Fourth Chamber

These are the instructions for the Third Chamber of the Fourth Hall of the Kingdom of Heaven.

As I experience the disintegration of my organic identity into the primal elements of consciousness in my passage through the eternal world, the tattered remnants of the world of matter surround me.

These apparitions of phenomena are my own evocations, emanating from my own primordial consciousness.

In the Third Chamber of the Fourth Hall, the phantom reverberations of my organic identity are consumed in the significance of organic fear, evoking illusions of the phenomenal world, and my attention is caught up in this distraction.

I remember the significance of organic fear in my passage through the phenomenal world and, passing once again into the endless emptiness of the Void, this significance swirls upward in my consciousness. Not swept away by it into the magnetic force of sudden rebirth, I invoke the presence of the guardian of the Third Chamber of the Fourth Hall of Heaven, the angel Rikbiel, who is a chief of the Order of *Galgalim* with six other angels, and who is above Metatron as a great crown prince of the Day of Judgment, appointed ruler of the Divine Chariot of Fire; the angel Rikbiel I invoke.

Brilliant white radiation emanates from his heart, penetrating and dissolving all reverberations of organic fear. At the same time, the phantom after-images of the phenomenal world, bathed in soft, smoky black light, seem to offer refuge from the cleansing radiation.

Not becoming engulfed in the seductive magnetic force of rebirth, I bathe in cleansing radiation, the brilliant white light dissolving all reverberations of the organic mind.

Wandering in the phantom images of the organic world, may my non-phenomenal self be cleansed by the brilliant radiation of the angel Rikbiel; may inexorable reality be my guide.

May I remain impartial to phenomena, free from organic significance, not expelled in sudden rebirth.

May the blessed angel Rikbiel be my protector. May he bring me safely through the Third Chamber of the Fourth Hall which is his domain. May he help me to remember my non-phenomenal self.

Involved with significance of anxious expectation,
Swelling upward from my hidden self,
Separating into primal form,
Illusion of phenomena.

Opening before me paths of fear and anger,
Nothing there but misery and pain,
Serene and calm I wait in stillness and in silence,
Bathed in cleansing radiation.

Brilliant in the light of inner vision,
I see myself wreathed in seething hate,
Offering no sympathy or help,
Tantalizingly superior.

Penetrating radiation,
White explosion from his heart to mine,
Another light, soft black, near the first,
Seems to offer refuge to my soul.

Melting in vibrating fusion,
Dissolving my resistance,
I lose the force of my reactions,
Not attracted to the light of smoky black.

Wandering alone in worlds of fear,
Bathed in cleansing radiation,
Surrendering myself
In endless crystal waters.

All phenomena is illusion,
Neither attracted nor repelled,
Not making any sudden moves,
My habits will carry me through.

Twenty-Fifth Chamber

These are the instructions for the Fourth Chamber of the Fourth Hall of the Kingdom of Heaven.

As I experience the disintegration of my organic identity into the primal elements of consciousness in my passage through the eternal world, the tattered remnants of the world of matter surround me.

These apparitions of phenomena are my own evocations, emanating from my own primordial consciousness.

In the Fourth Chamber of the Fourth Hall, the phantom reverberations of organic fear are consumed in the significance of organic jealousy, evoking illusions of the phenomenal world, and my attention is caught up in this distraction.

I remember the significance of organic jealousy in my passage through the phenomenal world and, passing once again into the endless emptiness of the Void, this significance swirls upward in my consciousness. Not swept away by it into the magnetic force of sudden rebirth, I invoke the presence of the guardian of the Fourth Chamber of the Fourth Hall of Heaven, the angel Sopheriel, who is appointed recording angel over the books of the living and the dead, scribe and keeper of records who shall present the souls of men and women on the Day of Judgment; the angel Sopheriel I invoke.

Brilliant green radiation emanates from his heart, penetrating and dissolving all reverberations of organic jealousy. At the same time, the phantom after-images of the phenomenal world, bathed in soft, smoky red light, seem to offer refuge from the cleansing radiation.

Not becoming engulfed in the seductive magnetic force of rebirth, I bathe in cleansing radiation, the brilliant green light dissolving all reverberations of the organic mind.

Wandering in the phantom images of the organic world, may my non-phenomenal self be cleansed by the brilliant radiation of the angel Sopheriel; may inexorable reality be my guide.

May I remain impartial to phenomena, free from organic significance, not expelled in sudden rebirth.

May the blessed angel Sopheriel be my protector. May he bring me safely through the Fourth Chamber of the Fourth Hall which is his domain. May he help me to remember my non-phenomenal self.

Involved with significance of jealousy and competition,
Rising upward from my hidden self,
Separating into primal form,
Repulsively attractive.

Opening before me paths of lingering uncertainty,
Nothing there but misery and pain,
Serene and calm I wait in stillness and in silence,
Bathed in cleansing radiation.

Brilliant in the light of inner vision,
I see myself suspiciously distrustful,
Clinging to my every action,
Gnawing at my soul.

Penetrating radiation,
Green explosion from his heart to mine,
Another light, soft red, near the first,
Seems to offer refuge to my soul.

Melting in vibrating fusion,
Dissolving my resistance,
I lose the force of my reactions,
Not attracted to the soft red light.

Wandering alone in worlds of jealousy,
Bathed in cleansing radiation,
Surrendering myself
In endless crystal waters.

All phenomena is illusion,
Neither attracted nor repelled,
Not making any sudden moves,
My habits will carry me through.

Twenty-Sixth Chamber

These are the instructions for the Fifth Chamber of the Fourth Hall of the Kingdom of Heaven.

As I experience the disintegration of my organic identity into the primal elements of consciousness in my passage through the eternal world, the tattered remnants of the world of matter surround me.

These apparitions of phenomena are my own evocations, emanating from my own primordial consciousness.

In the Fourth Chamber of the Fourth Hall, the phantom reverberations of organic jealousy are consumed in the significance of organic self-pity, evoking illusions of the phenomenal world, and my attention is caught up in this distraction.

I remember the significance of organic self-pity in my passage through the phenomenal world and, passing once again into the endless emptiness of the Void, this significance swirls upward in my consciousness. Not swept away by it into the magnetic force of sudden rebirth, I invoke the presence of the guardian of the Fifth Chamber of the Fourth Hall of Heaven, the angel Shemuel, who is called the Divine Name of God, the mighty angel who listens at the windows of the Mansion of Heaven to the songs of praise and devotion ascending from the temples of prayer in the phenomenal world and who is a great celestial Archon; the angel Shemuel I invoke.

Brilliant yellow radiation emanates from his heart, penetrating and dissolving all reverberations of organic self-pity. At the same time, the phantom after-images of the phenomenal world, bathed in soft, smoky blue light, seem to offer refuge from the cleansing radiation.

Not becoming engulfed in the seductive magnetic force of rebirth, I bathe in cleansing radiation, the brilliant yellow light dissolving all reverberations of the organic mind.

Wandering in the phantom images of the organic world, may my non-phenomenal self be cleansed by the brilliant radiation of the angel Shemuel; may inexorable reality be my guide.

May I remain impartial to phenomena, free from organic significance, not expelled in sudden rebirth.

May the blessed angel Shemuel be my protector. May he bring me safely through the Fifth Chamber of the Fourth Hall which is his domain. May he help me to remember my non-phenomenal self.

Involved with significance of vanity and arrogance,
Towering above myself in pride,
Separating into primal form,
Immovably secure.

Opening before me paths of isolation,
Nothing there but misery and pain,
Serene and calm I wait in stillness and in silence,
Bathed in cleansing radiation.

Brilliant in the light of inner vision,
I see myself inferior and foolish,
Holding tightly to the past and present,
Terrified to bend.

Penetrating radiation,
Yellow explosion from his heart to mine,
Another light, soft blue, near the first,
Seems to offer refuge to my soul.

Melting in vibrating fusion,
Dissolving my resistance,
I lose the force of my reactions,
Not attracted to the soft blue light.

Wandering alone in worlds of pride,
Bathed in cleansing radiation,
Surrendering myself
In endless crystal waters.

All phenomena is illusion,
Neither attracted nor repelled,
Not making any sudden moves,
My habits will carry me through.

Twenty-Seventh Chamber

These are the instructions for the Sixth Chamber of the Fourth hall of the Kingdom of Heaven.

As I experience the disintegration of my organic identity into the primal elements of consciousness in my passage through the eternal world, the tattered remnants of the world of matter surround me.

These apparitions of phenomena are my own evocations, emanating from my own primordial consciousness.

In the Sixth Chamber of the Fourth Hall, the phantom reverberations of organic self-pity are consumed in the significance of organic hunger, evoking illusions of the phenomenal world, and my attention is caught up in this distraction.

I remember the significance of organic hunger in my passage through the phenomenal world and, passing once again into the endless emptiness of the Void, this significance swirls upward in my consciousness. Not swept away by it into the magnetic force of sudden rebirth, I invoke the presence of the guardian of the Sixth Chamber of the Fourth Hall of Heaven, the angel Sariel, one of the great archangels, angel of the Summer Solstice who governs the sign of Aries and teaches the courses of the lunar world, who is guardian of the Third Tower of Heaven, a commander of the forces of fire and air; the angel Sariel I invoke.

Brilliant red radiation emanates from his heart, penetrating and dissolving all reverberations of organic hunger. At the same time, the phantom after-images of the phenomenal world, bathed in soft, smoky yellow light, seem to offer refuge from the cleansing radiation.

Not becoming engulfed in the seductive magnetic force of rebirth, I bathe in cleansing radiation, the brilliant red light dissolving all reverberations of the organic mind.

Wandering in the phantom images of the organic world, may my non-phenomenal self be cleansed by the brilliant radiation of the angel Sariel; may inexorable reality be my guide.

May I remain impartial to phenomena, free from organic significance, not expelled in sudden rebirth.

May the blessed angel Sariel be my protector. May he bring me safely through the Sixth Chamber of the Fourth Hall which is his domain. May he help me to remember my non-phenomenal self.

Involved with significance of passionate possession,
Liberated from illusion of phenomena,
Separating into primal form,
Phenomena of senses.

Opening before me paths of endless passion,
Nothing there but misery and pain,
Serene and calm I wait in stillness and in silence,
Bathed in cleansing radiation.

Brilliant in the light of inner vision,
I see myself seductive and compelling,
Searching endlessly for satisfaction,
Always wanting more.

Penetrating radiation,
Red explosion from his heart to mine,
Another light, soft yellow, near the first,
Seems to offer refuge to my soul.

Melting in vibrating fusion,
Dissolving my resistance,
I lose the force of my reactions,
Not attracted to the yellow light.

Wandering alone among the hungry souls,
Bathed in cleansing radiation,
Surrendering myself
In endless crystal waters.

All phenomena is illusion,
Neither attracted nor repelled,
Not making any sudden moves,
My habits will carry me through.

Twenty-Eighth Chamber

These are the instructions for the Seventh Chamber of the Fourth Hall of the Kingdom of Heaven.

As I experience the disintegration of my organic identity into the primal elements of consciousness in my passage through the eternal world, the tattered remnants of the world of matter surround me.

These apparitions of phenomena are my own evocations, emanating from my own primordial consciousness.

In the Seventh Chamber of the Fourth Hall, the phantom reverberations of organic hunger are consumed in the significance of organic compulsions, evoking illusions of the phenomenal world, and my attention is caught up in this distraction.

I remember the significance of organic compulsions in my passage through the phenomenal world and, passing once again into the endless emptiness of the Void, this significance swirls upward in my consciousness. Not swept away by it into the magnetic force of sudden rebirth, I invoke the presence of the guardian of the Seventh Chamber of the Fourth Hall of Heaven, the angel Suriel, who is called He Who Follows God's Commands, prince of the presence of the Absolute, angel of death who transported the soul of Moses to Heaven in which he resides, one of the four primordial archangels, one of the four angelic rulers of Earth, whose mantle covers the fixed stars, the source of Moses' knowledge, who brought Adam and Eve from the top of the mountain where Satan had lured them to the cave of treasures, who keeps watch in the days before the final judgment, who presides over the Solar System, ruler of the sign of Leo; the angel Suriel I invoke.

Brilliant orange radiation emanates from his heart, penetrating and dissolving all reverberations of organic compulsions. At the same time, the phantom after-images of the phenomenal world, bathed in soft, smoky violet light, seem to offer refuge from the cleansing radiation.

Not becoming engulfed in the seductive magnetic force of rebirth, I bathe in cleansing radiation, the brilliant orange light dissolving all reverberations of the organic mind.

Wandering in the phantom images of the organic world, may my non-phenomenal self be cleansed by the brilliant radiation of the angel Suriel; may inexorable reality be my guide.

May I remain impartial to phenomena, free from organic significance, not expelled in sudden rebirth.

May the blessed angel Suriel be my protector. May he bring me safely through the Seventh Chamber of the Fourth Hall which is his domain. May he help me to remember my non-phenomenal self.

Involved with significance of my compulsive actions,
Swirling in a hurricane of force,
Separating into primal elements,
Phenomena of consciousness.

Opening before me paths of inattention,
Nothing there but misery and pain,
Serene and calm I wait in stillness and in silence,
Bathed in cleansing radiation.

Brilliant in the light of inner vision,
I see myself so comfortably familiar,
Master of all space and time,
Manifesting all phenomena.

Penetrating radiation,
Orange explosion from his heart to mine,
Another light, soft violet, near the first,
Seems to offer refuge to my soul.

Melting in vibrating fusion,
Dissolving my resistance,
I lose the force of my reactions,
Not attracted to the violet light.

Wandering alone in worlds of habit,
Bathed in cleansing radiation,
Surrendering myself
In endless crystal waters.

All phenomena is illusion,
Neither attracted nor repelled,
Not making any sudden moves,
My habits will carry me through.

Fifth Hall

In the Fifth Hall everything is shattered into fragments and yet it is one single Living Being who is beyond unity and fragmentation. If a mirror were to reflect only itself, what would it see?

When that which is invisible is reduced to nothing, what is there to see?

The phenomenal world is like a house of wax, adorned with a thousand colors. If the wax is heated, all the colors and shapes run together and the forms I admire are worthless.

When I entered this hall I vanished from sight; everything in my vision is part of the unity of the King. I am silent when He speaks, and speak when He is silent.

In the mirrored sphere of the Fifth Hall I see only the face of the Beloved. Of myself, I see nothing.

Twenty-Ninth Chamber

These are the instructions for the First Chamber of the Fifth Hall of the Kingdom of Heaven.

As I experience the disintegration of my organic identity into the primal elements of consciousness in my passage through the eternal world, the tattered remnants of the world of matter surround me.

These apparitions of phenomena are my own evocations, emanating from my own primordial consciousness.

In the First Chamber of the Fifth Hall, the phantom reverberations of organic compulsions are consumed in sensations of the organic mind, evoking illusions of the phenomenal world, and my attention is caught up in this distraction.

I remember the sensations of the organic mind in my passage through the phenomenal world and, passing once again into the endless emptiness of the Void, these sensations swirl upward in my consciousness. Not swept away by them into the magnetic force of sudden rebirth, I invoke the presence of the guardian of the First Chamber of the Fifth Hall of Heaven, the angel Mihriel, the angel of friendship and love, who stands on the bridge of Sirat which is finer than a hair and sharper than a sword, to examine every spirit who wishes to cross; who with a balance weighs the spirit's actions performed in the phenomenal world, and allows him to pass if his phenomenal activities are too slight to interrupt the flow of force and, if too great, hurls him back to the phenomenal world. He who has one thousand ears and ten thousand eyes, the angel Mihriel I invoke.

Brilliant violet radiation emanates from his heart, penetrating and dissolving all reverberations of the organic mind. At the same time, the phantom after-images of the phenomenal world, bathed in soft, smoky orange light, seem to offer refuge from the cleansing radiation.

Not becoming engulfed in the seductive magnetic force of rebirth, I bathe in cleansing radiation, the brilliant violet light dissolving all reverberations of the organic mind.

Wandering in the phantom images of the organic world, may my non-phenomenal self be cleansed by the brilliant radiation of the angel Mihriel; may inexorable reality be my guide.

May I remain impartial to phenomena, free from organic sensations, not expelled in sudden rebirth.

May the blessed angel Mihriel be my protector. May he bring me safely through the First Chamber of the Fifth Hall which is his domain. May he help me to remember my non-phenomenal self.

Involved with sensations of solid form,
Swirling in a hurricane of force,
Separating into primal elements,
Phenomena of motion.

Opening before me paths of flesh and blood,
Nothing there but misery and pain,
Serene and calm I wait in stillness and in silence,
Bathed in cleansing radiation.

Brilliant in the light of inner vision,
I see my ego struggling for breath,
Clinging tightly to the remnants of organic life,
Terrified to die.

Penetrating radiation,
Violet explosion from his heart to mine,
Another light, soft orange, near the first,
Seems to offer refuge to my soul.

Melting in vibrating fusion,
Dissolving my resistance,
I lose the force of my reactions,
Not attracted to the orange light.

Wandering alone, maintaining sensations of body symptoms,
Bathed in cleansing radiation,
Surrendering myself
In endless crystal waters.

All phenomena is illusion,
Neither attracted nor repelled,
Not making any sudden moves,
My habits will carry me through.

Thirtieth Chamber

These are the instructions for the Second Chamber of the Fifth Hall of the Kingdom of Heaven.

As I experience the disintegration of my organic identity into the primal elements of consciousness in my passage through the eternal world, the tattered remnants of the world of matter surround me.

These apparitions of phenomena are my own evocations, emanating from my own primordial consciousness.

In the Second Chamber of the Fifth Hall, the phantom reverberations of the organic mind are consumed in sensations of my organic identity, evoking illusions of the phenomenal world, and my attention is caught up in this distraction.

I remember the sensations of my organic identity in my passage through the phenomenal world and, passing once again into the endless emptiness of the Void, these sensations swirl upward in my consciousness. Not swept away by them into the magnetic force of sudden rebirth, I invoke the presence of the guardian of the Second Chamber of the Fifth Hall of Heaven, the angel Azza, suspended between Heaven and Earth, who had carnal knowledge of mortal women in the phenomenal world, who falls forever between the inner and outer worlds, who revealed to Solomon the higher arcana and gave him wisdom; the angel Azza I invoke.

Brilliant blue radiation emanates from his heart, penetrating and dissolving all reverberations of my organic identity. At the same time, the phantom after-images of the phenomenal world, bathed in soft, smoky white light, seem to offer refuge from the cleansing radiation.

Not becoming engulfed in the seductive magnetic force of rebirth, I bathe in cleansing radiation, the brilliant blue light dissolving all reverberations of the organic mind.

Wandering in the phantom images of the organic world, may my non-phenomenal self be cleansed by the brilliant radiation of the angel Azza; may inexorable reality be my guide.

May I remain impartial to phenomena, free from organic sensations, not expelled in sudden rebirth.

May the blessed angel Azza be my protector. May he bring me safely through the Second Chamber of the Fifth Hall which is his domain. May he help me to remember my non-phenomenal self.

Involved with sensations of my identity,
Swirling in a hurricane of force,
Separating into primal elements,
Phenomena of dimension.

Opening before me paths of time and space,
Nothing there but misery and pain,
Serene and calm I wait in stillness and in silence,
Bathed in cleansing radiation.

Brilliant in the light of inner vision,
I see myself controlling destiny,
Clinging to the content of the mind,
Frozen memory.

Penetrating radiation,
Blue explosion from his heart to mine,
Another light, soft white, near the first,
Seems to offer refuge to my soul.

Melting in vibrating fusion,
Dissolving my resistance,
I lose the force of my reactions,
Not attracted to the soft white light.

Wandering alone, maintaining sensations of ego,
Bathed in cleansing radiation,
Surrendering myself
In endless crystal waters.

All phenomena is illusion,
Neither attracted nor repelled,
Not making any sudden moves,
My habits will carry me through.

Thirty-First Chamber

These are the instructions for the Third Chamber of the Fifth Hall of the Kingdom of Heaven.

As I experience the disintegration of my organic identity into the primal elements of consciousness in my passage through the eternal world, the tattered remnants of the world of matter surround me.

These apparitions of phenomena are my own evocations, emanating from my own primordial consciousness.

In the Third Chamber of the Fifth Hall, the phantom reverberations of my organic identity are consumed in sensations of organic fear, evoking illusions of the phenomenal world, and my attention is caught up in this distraction.

I remember the sensations of organic fear in my passage through the phenomenal world and, passing once again into the endless emptiness of the Void, these sensations swirl upward in my consciousness. Not swept away by them into the magnetic force of sudden rebirth, I invoke the presence of the guardian of the Third Chamber of the Fifth Hall of Heaven, the angel Uriel, who binds the passive and holds them until the Day of Judgment, who governs the sign of Virgo and governs fifty myriads of angels fashioned by the Lord from fire and water, subordinate of Jehoel, the prince of fire; the angel Uriel I invoke.

Brilliant white radiation emanates from his heart, penetrating and dissolving all reverberations of organic fear. At the same time, the phantom after-images of the phenomenal world, bathed in soft, smoky black light, seem to offer refuge from the cleansing radiation.

Not becoming engulfed in the seductive magnetic force of rebirth, I bathe in cleansing radiation, the brilliant white light dissolving all reverberations of the organic mind.

Wandering in the phantom images of the organic world, may my non-phenomenal self be cleansed by the brilliant radiation of the angel Uriel; may inexorable reality be my guide.

May I remain impartial to phenomena, free from organic sensations, not expelled in sudden rebirth.

May the blessed angel Uriel be my protector. May he bring me safely through the Third Chamber of the Fifth Hall which is his domain. May he help me to remember my non-phenomenal self.

Involved with sensations of anxious expectation,
Swelling upward from my hidden self,
Separating into primal form,
Illusion of phenomena.

Opening before me paths of fear and anger,
Nothing there but misery and pain,
Serene and calm I wait in stillness and in silence,
Bathed in cleansing radiation.

Brilliant in the light of inner vision,
I see myself wreathed in seething hate,
Offering no sympathy or help,
Tantalizingly superior.

Penetrating radiation,
White explosion from his heart to mine,
Another light, soft black, near the first,
Seems to offer refuge to my soul.

Melting in vibrating fusion,
Dissolving my resistance,
I lose the force of my reactions,
Not attracted to the light of smoky black.

Wandering alone in worlds of fear,
Bathed in cleansing radiation,
Surrendering myself
In endless crystal waters.

All phenomena is illusion,
Neither attracted nor repelled,
Not making any sudden moves,
My habits will carry me through.

Thirty-Second Chamber

These are the instructions for the Fourth Chamber of the Fifth Hall of the Kingdom of Heaven.

As I experience the disintegration of my organic identity into the primal elements of consciousness in my passage through the eternal world, the tattered remnants of the world of matter surround me.

These apparitions of phenomena are my own evocations, emanating from my own primordial consciousness.

In the Fourth Chamber of the Fifth Hall, the phantom reverberations of organic fear are consumed in sensations of organic jealousy, evoking illusions of the phenomenal world, and my attention is caught up in this distraction.

I remember the sensations of organic jealousy in my passage through the phenomenal world and, passing once again into the endless emptiness of the Void, these sensations swirl upward in my consciousness. Not swept away by them into the magnetic force of sudden rebirth, I invoke the presence of the guardian of the Fourth Chamber of the Fifth Hall of Heaven, the angel Israfel, the burning angel of resurrection and of song, who blows the trumpet on Judgment Day, whose feet are under the Earth but whose head reaches to the pillars of the Divine Throne, who six times each day allows his vision to penetrate the world of Hell, who was sent to the four corners of the Earth to obtain dust for the creation of the First Adam, and who is to be destroyed by fire at the end of the phenomenal world, whose heart and voice emanate the sweetest sounds of all the creations of God; the angel Israfel I invoke.

Brilliant green radiation emanates from his heart, penetrating and dissolving all reverberations of organic jealousy. At the same time, the phantom after-images of the phenomenal world, bathed in soft, smoky red light, seem to offer refuge from the cleansing radiation.

Not becoming engulfed in the seductive magnetic force of rebirth, I bathe in cleansing radiation, the brilliant green light dissolving all reverberations of the organic mind.

Wandering in the phantom images of the organic world, may my non-phenomenal self be cleansed by the brilliant radiation of the angel Israfel; may inexorable reality be my guide.

May I remain impartial to phenomena, free from organic sensations, not expelled in sudden rebirth.

May the blessed angel Israfel be my protector. May he bring me safely through the Fourth Chamber of the Fifth Hall which is his domain. May he help me to remember my non-phenomenal self.

Involved with sensations of jealousy and competition,
Rising upward from my hidden self,
Separating into primal form,
Repulsively attractive.

Opening before me paths of lingering uncertainty,
Nothing there but misery and pain,
Serene and calm I wait in stillness and in silence,
Bathed in cleansing radiation.

Brilliant in the light of inner vision,
I see myself suspiciously distrustful,
Clinging to my every action,
Gnawing at my soul.

Penetrating radiation,
Green explosion from his heart to mine,
Another light, soft red, near the first,
Seems to offer refuge to my soul.

Melting in vibrating fusion,
Dissolving my resistance,
I lose the force of my reactions,
Not attracted to the soft red light.

Wandering alone in worlds of jealousy,
Bathed in cleansing radiation,
Surrendering myself
In endless crystal waters.

All phenomena is illusion,
Neither attracted nor repelled,
Not making any sudden moves,
My habits will carry me through.

Thirty-Third Chamber

These are the instructions for the Fifth Chamber of the Fifth Hall of the Kingdom of Heaven.

As I experience the disintegration of my organic identity into the primal elements of consciousness in my passage through the eternal world, the tattered remnants of the world of matter surround me.

These apparitions of phenomena are my own evocations, emanating from my own primordial consciousness.

In the Fifth Chamber of the Fifth Hall, the phantom reverberations of organic jealousy are consumed in sensations of organic self-pity, evoking illusions of the phenomenal world, and my attention is caught up in this distraction.

I remember the sensations of organic self-pity in my passage through the phenomenal world and, passing once again into the endless emptiness of the Void, these sensations swirl upward in my consciousness. Not swept away by them into the magnetic force of sudden rebirth, I invoke the presence of the guardian of the Fifth Chamber of the Fifth Hall of Heaven, the angel Israel, who strives with the Lord God and surrounds his Throne, angel of the Order of *Hayyoth*, archangel of the power of God and chief tribune among the sons of God, who appeared on Earth as the patriarch Jacob and entered the phenomenal world as a prophet and messenger of God; the angel Israel I invoke.

Brilliant yellow radiation emanates from his heart, penetrating and dissolving all reverberations of organic self-pity. At the same time, the phantom after-images of the phenomenal world, bathed in soft, smoky blue light, seem to offer refuge from the cleansing radiation.

Not becoming engulfed in the seductive magnetic force of rebirth, I bathe in cleansing radiation, the brilliant yellow light dissolving all reverberations of the organic mind.

Wandering in the phantom images of the organic world, may my non-phenomenal self be cleansed by the brilliant radiation of the angel Israel; may inexorable reality be my guide.

May I remain impartial to phenomena, free from organic sensations, not expelled in sudden rebirth.

May the blessed angel Israel be my protector. May he bring me safely through the Fifth Chamber of the Fifth Hall which is his domain. May he help me to remember my non-phenomenal self.

Involved with sensations of vanity and arrogance,
Towering above myself in pride,
Separating into primal form,
Immovably secure.

Opening before me paths of isolation,
Nothing there but misery and pain,
Serene and calm I wait in stillness and in silence,
Bathed in cleansing radiation.

Brilliant in the light of inner vision,
I see myself inferior and foolish,
Holding tightly to the past and present,
Terrified to bend.

Penetrating radiation,
Yellow explosion from his heart to mine,
Another light, soft blue, near the first,
Seems to offer refuge to my soul.

Melting in vibrating fusion,
Dissolving my resistance,
I lose the force of my reactions,
Not attracted to the soft blue light.

Wandering alone in worlds of pride,
Bathed in cleansing radiation,
Surrendering myself
In endless crystal waters.

All phenomena is illusion,
Neither attracted nor repelled,
Not making any sudden moves,
My habits will carry me through.

Thirty-Fourth Chamber

These are the instructions for the Sixth Chamber of the Fifth Hall of the Kingdom of Heaven.

As I experience the disintegration of my organic identity into the primal elements of consciousness in my passage through the eternal world, the tattered remnants of the world of matter surround me.

These apparitions of phenomena are my own evocations, emanating from my own primordial consciousness.

In the Sixth Chamber of the Fifth Hall, the phantom reverberations of organic self-pity are consumed in sensations of organic hunger, evoking illusions of the phenomenal world, and my attention is caught up in this distraction.

I remember the sensations of organic hunger in my passage through the phenomenal world and, passing once again into the endless emptiness of the Void, these sensations swirl upward in my consciousness. Not swept away by them into the magnetic force of sudden rebirth, I invoke the presence of the guardian of the Sixth Chamber of the Fifth Hall of Heaven, the angel Zagiel, he of the Divine Splendor, prince of the Holy Law and the hand of wisdom of the ancients, who instructed Moses in the Ineffable Name of God, the angel of the burning bush on the Mount of Sinai, chief guardian of the chambers of the Citadel of Heaven, prince of the Holy Presence of the Absolute, who descended with Michael and Gabriel when they took Moses up to Heaven; the angel Zagiel I invoke.

Brilliant red radiation emanates from his heart, penetrating and dissolving all reverberations of organic hunger. At the same time, the phantom after-images of the phenomenal world, bathed in soft, smoky yellow light, seem to offer refuge from the cleansing radiation.

Not becoming engulfed in the seductive magnetic force of rebirth, I bathe in cleansing radiation, the brilliant red light dissolving all reverberations of the organic mind.

Wandering in the phantom images of the organic world, may my non-phenomenal self be cleansed by the brilliant radiation of the angel Zagiel; may inexorable reality be my guide.

May I remain impartial to phenomena, free from organic sensations, not expelled in sudden rebirth.

May the blessed angel Zagiel be my protector. May he bring me safely through the Sixth Chamber of the Fifth Hall which is his domain. May he help me to remember my non-phenomenal self.

Involved with sensations of passionate possession,
Liberated from illusion of phenomena,
Separating into primal form,
Phenomena of senses.

Opening before me paths of endless passion,
Nothing there but misery and pain,
Serene and calm I wait in stillness and in silence,
Bathed in cleansing radiation.

Brilliant in the light of inner vision,
I see myself seductive and compelling,
Searching endlessly for satisfaction,
Always wanting more.

Penetrating radiation,
Red explosion from his heart to mine,
Another light, soft yellow, near the first,
Seems to offer refuge to my soul.

Melting in vibrating fusion,
Dissolving my resistance,
I lose the force of my reactions,
Not attracted to the yellow light.

Wandering alone among the hungry souls,
Bathed in cleansing radiation,
Surrendering myself
In endless crystal waters.

All phenomena is illusion,
Neither attracted nor repelled,
Not making any sudden moves,
My habits will carry me through.

Thirty-Fifth Chamber

These are the instructions for the Seventh Chamber of the Fifth Hall of the Kingdom of Heaven.

As I experience the disintegration of my organic identity into the primal elements of consciousness in my passage through the eternal world, the tattered remnants of the world of matter surround me.

These apparitions of phenomena are my own evocations, emanating from my own primordial consciousness.

In the Seventh Chamber of the Fifth Hall, the phantom reverberations of organic hunger are consumed in sensations of organic compulsions, evoking illusions of the phenomenal world, and my attention is caught up in this distraction.

I remember the sensations of organic compulsions in my passage through the phenomenal world and, passing once again into the endless emptiness of the Void, these sensations swirl upward in my consciousness. Not swept away by them into the magnetic force of sudden rebirth, I invoke the presence of the guardian of the Seventh Chamber of the Fifth Hall of Heaven, the angel Araquiel, who teaches the signs of the Earth and leads the souls of men and women to the judgment chamber, who exercises dominion over the Earth, one of the seven holy angels who protect the souls of children whose parents have sinned; the angel Araquiel I invoke.

Brilliant orange radiation emanates from his heart, penetrating and dissolving all reverberations of organic compulsions. At the same time, the phantom after-images of the phenomenal world, bathed in soft, smoky violet light, seem to offer refuge from the cleansing radiation.

Not becoming engulfed in the seductive magnetic force of rebirth, I bathe in cleansing radiation, the brilliant orange light dissolving all reverberations of the organic mind.

Wandering in the phantom images of the organic world, may my non-phenomenal self be cleansed by the brilliant radiation of the angel Araquiel; may inexorable reality be my guide.

May I remain impartial to phenomena, free from organic sensations, not expelled in sudden rebirth.

May the blessed angel Araquiel be my protector. May he bring me safely through the Seventh Chamber of the Fifth Hall which is his domain. May he help me to remember my non-phenomenal self.

Involved with sensations of my compulsive actions,
Swirling in a hurricane of force,
Separating into primal elements,
Phenomena of consciousness.

Opening before me paths of inattention,
Nothing there but misery and pain,
Serene and calm I wait in stillness and in silence,
Bathed in cleansing radiation.

Brilliant in the light of inner vision,
I see myself so comfortably familiar,
Master of all space and time,
Manifesting all phenomena.

Penetrating radiation,
Orange explosion from his heart to mine,
Another light, soft violet, near the first,
Seems to offer refuge to my soul.

Melting in vibrating fusion,
Dissolving my resistance,
I lose the force of my reactions,
Not attracted to the violet light.

Wandering alone in worlds of habit,
Bathed in cleansing radiation,
Surrendering myself
In endless crystal waters.

All phenomena is illusion,
Neither attracted nor repelled,
Not making any sudden moves,
My habits will carry me through.

Sixth Hall

In the Sixth Hall, sounds of sighing, sorrow and lamenting fill the air, and yet through it all is an undercurrent of burning eagerness, the lover galvanized to meet the Beloved.

It is both day and night, light and dark, hot and cold. If I wonder whether or not I have existed, I cannot say, and yet I remember having existed.

If I wonder whether I am mortal or immortal, I cannot say, and yet I remember having been both mortal and immortal.

If I wonder whether my heart is full or empty, I sigh with bewilderment and astonishment and fall into the void.

Thirty-Sixth Chamber

These are the instructions for the First Chamber of the Sixth Hall of the Kingdom of Heaven.

As I experience the disintegration of my organic identity into the primal elements of consciousness in my passage through the eternal world, the tattered remnants of the world of matter surround me.

These apparitions of phenomena are my own evocations, emanating from my own primordial consciousness.

In the First Chamber of the Sixth Hall, the phantom reverberations of organic compulsions are consumed in manifestations of the organic mind, evoking illusions of the phenomenal world, and my attention is caught up in this distraction.

I remember the manifestations of the organic mind in my passage through the phenomenal world, and passing once again into the endless emptiness of the Void, these manifestations swirl upward in my consciousness. Not swept away by them into the magnetic force of sudden rebirth, I invoke the presence of the guardian of the First Chamber of the Sixth Hall of Heaven, the angel Azazel, to whom God gives strength, and who is one of the chiefs of the Order of *Bene Elim,* who cohabited with Naamah, Lamech's daughter and sired the *Sedim,* guardians of the spirits of wandering souls, guardian of hidden treasures and lost secrets, who was appointed by God to transcribe the two hundred and four books of Ezra, who taught men to fashion weapons and women the arts of seduction; the angel Azazel I invoke.

Brilliant violet radiation emanates from his heart, penetrating and dissolving all reverberations of the organic mind. At the same time, the phantom after-images of the phenomenal world, bathed in soft, smoky orange light, seem to offer refuge from the cleansing radiation.

Not becoming engulfed in the seductive magnetic force of rebirth, I bathe in cleansing radiation, the brilliant violet light dissolving all reverberations of the organic mind.

Wandering in the phantom images of the organic world, may my non-phenomenal self be cleansed by the brilliant radiation of the angel Azazel; may inexorable reality be my guide.

May I remain impartial to phenomena, free from organic manifestations, not expelled in sudden rebirth.

May the blessed angel Azazel be my protector. May he bring me safely through the First Chamber of the Sixth Hall which is his domain. May he help me to remember my non-phenomenal self.

Involved with manifestations of solid form,
Swirling in a hurricane of force,
Separating into primal elements,
Phenomena of motion.

Opening before me paths of flesh and blood,
Nothing there but misery and pain,
Serene and calm I wait in stillness and in silence,
Bathed in cleansing radiation.

Brilliant in the light of inner vision,
I see my ego struggling for breath,
Clinging tightly to the remnants of organic life,
Terrified to die.

Penetrating radiation,
Violet explosion from his heart to mine,
Another light, soft orange, near the first,
Seems to offer refuge to my soul.

Melting in vibrating fusion,
Dissolving my resistance,
I lose the force of my reactions,
Not attracted to the orange light.

Wandering alone, maintaining manifestations of body symptoms,
Bathed in cleansing radiation,
Surrendering myself
In endless crystal waters.

All phenomena is illusion,
Neither attracted nor repelled,
Not making any sudden moves,
My habits will carry me through.

Thirty-Seventh Chamber

These are the instructions for the Second Chamber of the Sixth Hall of the Kingdom of Heaven.

As I experience the disintegration of my organic identity into the primal elements of consciousness in my passage through the eternal world, the tattered remnants of the world of matter surround me.

These apparitions of phenomena are my own evocations, emanating from my own primordial consciousness.

In the Second Chamber of the Sixth Hall, the phantom reverberations of the organic mind are consumed in manifestations of my organic identity, evoking illusions of the phenomenal world, and my attention is caught up in this distraction.

I remember the manifestations of my organic identity in my passage through the phenomenal world and, passing once again into the endless emptiness of the Void, these manifestations swirl upward in my consciousness. Not swept away by them into the magnetic force of sudden rebirth, I invoke the presence of the guardian of the Second Chamber of the Sixth Hall of Heaven, the angel Penemu, who taught the art of writing with ink and paper, and teaches the children of men and women the bittersweet secrets of wisdom, whose invocation cures confusion and disorientation during the time he is invoked; the angel Penemu I invoke.

Brilliant blue radiation emanates from his heart, penetrating and dissolving all reverberations of my organic identity. At the same time, the phantom after-images of the phenomenal world, bathed in soft, smoky white light, seem to offer refuge from the cleansing radiation.

Not becoming engulfed in the seductive magnetic force of rebirth, I bathe in cleansing radiation, the brilliant blue light dissolving all reverberations of the organic mind.

Wandering in the phantom images of the organic world, may my non-phenomenal self be cleansed by the brilliant radiation of the angel Penemu; may inexorable reality be my guide.

May I remain impartial to phenomena, free from organic manifestations, not expelled in sudden rebirth.

May the blessed angel Penemu be my protector. May he bring me safely through the Second Chamber of the Sixth Hall which is his domain. May he help me to remember my non-phenomenal self.

Involved with manifestations of my identity,
Swirling in a hurricane of force,
Separating into primal elements,
Phenomena of dimension.

Opening before me paths of time and space,
Nothing there but misery and pain,
Serene and calm I wait in stillness and in silence,
Bathed in cleansing radiation.

Brilliant in the light of inner vision,
I see myself controlling destiny,
Clinging to the content of the mind,
Frozen memory.

Penetrating radiation,
Blue explosion from his heart to mine,
Another light, soft white, near the first,
Seems to offer refuge to my soul.

Melting in vibrating fusion,
Dissolving my resistance,
I lose the force of my reactions,
Not attracted to the soft white light.

Wandering alone, maintaining manifestations of ego,
Bathed in cleansing radiation,
Surrendering myself
In endless crystal waters.

All phenomena is illusion,
Neither attracted nor repelled,
Not making any sudden moves,
My habits will carry me through.

Thirty-Eighth Chamber

These are the instructions for the Third Chamber of the Sixth Hall of the Kingdom of Heaven.

As I experience the disintegration of my organic identity into the primal elements of consciousness in my passage through the eternal world, the tattered remnants of the world of matter surround me.

These apparitions of phenomena are my own evocations, emanating from my own primordial consciousness.

In the Third Chamber of the Sixth Hall, the phantom reverberations of my organic identity are consumed in manifestations of organic fear, evoking illusions of the phenomenal world, and my attention is caught up in this distraction.

I remember the manifestations of organic fear in my passage through the phenomenal world and, passing once again into the endless emptiness of the Void, these manifestations swirl upward in my consciousness. Not swept away by them into the magnetic force of sudden rebirth, I invoke the presence of the guardian of the Third Chamber of the Sixth Hall of Heaven, the angel Shamshiel, light of day, mighty ruler of the citadel of Heaven, a prince of paradise and guardian angel of the Garden of Eden, who conducted Moses through the Halls of Heaven while he was still of the phenomenal world; who crowns prayers and accompanies great prayers to the higher halls and teaches the signs of the solar world; who served as one of the two chief aids to Uriel when he bore his standard into battle with Satan, to whom the treasures and secrets of David and Solomon were given over when they ascended into Heaven; the angel Shamshiel I invoke.

Brilliant white radiation emanates from his heart, penetrating and dissolving all reverberations of organic fear. At the same time, the phantom after-images of the phenomenal world, bathed in soft, smoky black light, seem to offer refuge from the cleansing radiation.

Not becoming engulfed in the seductive magnetic force of rebirth, I bathe in cleansing radiation, the brilliant white light dissolving all reverberations of the organic mind.

Wandering in the phantom images of the organic world, may my non-phenomenal self be cleansed by the brilliant radiation of the angel Shamshiel; may inexorable reality be my guide.

May I remain impartial to phenomena, free from organic manifestations, not expelled in sudden rebirth.

May the blessed angel Shamshiel be my protector. May he bring me safely through the Third Chamber of the Sixth Hall which is his domain. May he help me to remember my non-phenomenal self.

Involved with manifestations of anxious expectation,
Swelling upward from my hidden self,
Separating into primal form,
Illusion of phenomena.

Opening before me paths of fear and anger,
Nothing there but misery and pain,
Serene and calm I wait in stillness and in silence,
Bathed in cleansing radiation.

Brilliant in the light of inner vision,
I see myself wreathed in seething hate,
Offering no sympathy or help,
Tantalizingly superior.

Penetrating radiation,
White explosion from his heart to mine,
Another light, soft black, near the first,
Seems to offer refuge to my soul.

Melting in vibrating fusion,
Dissolving my resistance,
I lose the force of my reactions,
Not attracted to the light of smoky black.

Wandering alone in worlds of fear,
Bathed in cleansing radiation,
Surrendering myself
In endless crystal waters.

All phenomena is illusion,
Neither attracted nor repelled,
Not making any sudden moves,
My habits will carry me through.

Involved with manifestations of jealousy and competition,
Rising upward from my hidden self,
Separating into primal form,
Repulsively attractive.

Opening before me paths of lingering uncertainty,
Nothing there but misery and pain,
Serene and calm I wait in stillness and in silence,
Bathed in cleansing radiation.

Brilliant in the light of inner vision,
I see myself suspiciously distrustful,
Clinging to my every action,
Gnawing at my soul.

Penetrating radiation,
Green explosion from his heart to mine,
Another light, soft red, near the first,
Seems to offer refuge to my soul.

Melting in vibrating fusion,
Dissolving my resistance,
I lose the force of my reactions,
Not attracted to the soft red light.

Wandering alone in worlds of jealousy,
Bathed in cleansing radiation,
Surrendering myself
In endless crystal waters.

All phenomena is illusion,
Neither attracted nor repelled,
Not making any sudden moves,
My habits will carry me through.

Fortieth Chamber

These are the instructions for the Fifth Chamber of the Sixth Hall of the Kingdom of Heaven.

As I experience the disintegration of my organic identity into the primal elements of consciousness in my passage through the eternal world, the tattered remnants of the world of matter surround me.

These apparitions of phenomena are my own evocations, emanating from my own primordial consciousness.

In the Fifth Chamber of the Sixth Hall, the phantom reverberations of organic jealousy are consumed in manifestations of organic self-pity, evoking illusions of the phenomenal world, and my attention is caught up in this distraction.

I remember the manifestations of organic self-pity in my passage through the phenomenal world and, passing once again into the endless emptiness of the Void, these manifestations swirl upward in my consciousness. Not swept away by them into the magnetic force of sudden rebirth, I invoke the presence of the guardian of the Fifth Chamber of the Sixth Hall of Heaven, the angel Abraxis, the supreme unknown, a prince of *Aeons,* who blesses the dead, and is the Archon ruler of the three hundred and sixty-five Halls of Heaven, mediator between the creatures of the phenomenal world and the world of invoked presences; the angel Abraxis I invoke.

Brilliant yellow radiation emanates from his heart, penetrating and dissolving all reverberations of organic self-pity. At the same time, the phantom after-images of the phenomenal world, bathed in soft, smoky blue light, seem to offer refuge from the cleansing radiation.

Not becoming engulfed in the seductive magnetic force of rebirth, I bathe in cleansing radiation, the brilliant yellow light dissolving all reverberations of the organic mind.

Wandering in the phantom images of the organic world, may my non-phenomenal self be cleansed by the brilliant radiation of the angel Abraxis; may inexorable reality be my guide.

May I remain impartial to phenomena, free from organic manifestations, not expelled in sudden rebirth.

May the blessed angel Abraxis be my protector. May he bring me safely through the Fifth Chamber of the Sixth Hall which is his domain. May he help me to remember my non-phenomenal self.

Involved with manifestations of vanity and arrogance,
Towering above myself in pride,
Separating into primal form,
Immovably secure.

Opening before me paths of isolation,
Nothing there but misery and pain,
Serene and calm I wait in stillness and in silence,
Bathed in cleansing radiation.

Brilliant in the light of inner vision,
I see myself inferior and foolish,
Holding tightly to the past and present,
Terrified to bend.

Penetrating radiation,
Yellow explosion from his heart to mine,
Another light, soft blue, near the first,
Seems to offer refuge to my soul.

Melting in vibrating fusion,
Dissolving my resistance,
I lose the force of my reactions,
Not attracted to the soft blue light.

Wandering alone in worlds of pride,
Bathed in cleansing radiation,
Surrendering myself
In endless crystal waters.

All phenomena is illusion,
Neither attracted nor repelled,
Not making any sudden moves,
My habits will carry me through.

Forty-First Chamber

These are the instructions for the Sixth Chamber of the Sixth Hall of the Kingdom of Heaven.

As I experience the disintegration of my organic identity into the primal elements of consciousness in my passage through the eternal world, the tattered remnants of the world of matter surround me.

These apparitions of phenomena are my own evocations, emanating from my own primordial consciousness.

In the Sixth Chamber of the Sixth Hall, the phantom reverberations of organic self-pity are consumed in manifestations of organic hunger, evoking illusions of the phenomenal world, and my attention is caught up in this distraction.

I remember the manifestations of organic hunger in my passage through the phenomenal world and, passing once again into the endless emptiness of the Void, these manifestations swirl upward in my consciousness. Not swept away by them into the magnetic force of sudden rebirth, I invoke the presence of the guardian of the Sixth Chamber of the Sixth Hall of Heaven, the angel Boel, who is called *God is in him,* one of seven exalted angels of the Throne resident in the highest Heaven, who holds the Key to the phenomenal world by means of which the Angelic Host is able to enter the Garden of Eden which is closed to all except at great need; the angel Boel I invoke.

Brilliant red radiation emanates from his heart, penetrating and dissolving all reverberations of organic hunger. At the same time, the phantom after-images of the phenomenal world, bathed in soft, smoky yellow light, seem to offer refuge from the cleansing radiation.

Not becoming engulfed in the seductive magnetic force of rebirth, I bathe in cleansing radiation, the brilliant red light dissolving all reverberations of the organic mind.

Wandering in the phantom images of the organic world, may my non-phenomenal self be cleansed by the brilliant radiation of the angel Boel; may inexorable reality be my guide.

May I remain impartial to phenomena, free from organic manifestations, not expelled in sudden rebirth.

May the blessed angel Boel be my protector. May he bring me safely through the Sixth Chamber of the Sixth Hall which is his domain. May he help me to remember my non-phenomenal self.

Involved with manifestations of passionate possession,
Liberated from illusion of phenomena,
Separating into primal form,
Phenomena of senses.

Opening before me paths of endless passion,
Nothing there but misery and pain,
Serene and calm I wait in stillness and in silence,
Bathed in cleansing radiation.

Brilliant in the light of inner vision,
I see myself seductive and compelling,
Searching endlessly for satisfaction,
Always wanting more.

Penetrating radiation,
Red explosion from his heart to mine,
Another light, soft yellow, near the first,
Seems to offer refuge to my soul.

Melting in vibrating fusion,
Dissolving my resistance,
I lose the force of my reactions,
Not attracted to the yellow light.

Wandering alone among the hungry souls,
Bathed in cleansing radiation,
Surrendering myself
In endless crystal waters.

All phenomena is illusion,
Neither attracted nor repelled,
Not making any sudden moves,
My habits will carry me through.

Forty-Second Chamber

These are the instructions for the Seventh Chamber of the Sixth Hall of the Kingdom of Heaven.

As I experience the disintegration of my organic identity into the primal elements of consciousness in my passage through the eternal world, the tattered remnants of the world of matter surround me.

These apparitions of phenomena are my own evocations, emanating from my own primordial consciousness.

In the Seventh Chamber of the Sixth Hall, the phantom reverberations of organic hunger are consumed in manifestations of organic compulsions, evoking illusions of the phenomenal world, and my attention is caught up in this distraction.

I remember the manifestations of organic compulsions in my passage through the phenomenal world and, passing once again into the endless emptiness of the Void, these manifestations swirl upward in my consciousness. Not swept away by them into the magnetic force of sudden rebirth, I invoke the presence of the guardian of the Seventh Chamber of the Sixth Hall of Heaven, the angel Gazardiel, chief angelic supervisor of the East Halls, who kisses the prayers of the faithful and conveys them to the non-phenomenal world, and who holds the keys to light and darkness in the phenomenal world; the angel Gazardiel I invoke.

Brilliant orange radiation emanates from his heart, penetrating and dissolving all reverberations of organic compulsions. At the same time, the phantom after-images of the phenomenal world, bathed in soft, smoky violet light, seem to offer refuge from the cleansing radiation.

Not becoming engulfed in the seductive magnetic force of rebirth, I bathe in cleansing radiation, the brilliant orange light dissolving all reverberations of the organic mind.

Wandering in the phantom images of the organic world, may my non-phenomenal self be cleansed by the brilliant radiation of the angel Gazardiel; may inexorable reality be my guide.

May I remain impartial to phenomena, free from organic manifestations, not expelled in sudden rebirth.

May the blessed angel Gazardiel be my protector. May he bring me safely through the Seventh Chamber of the Sixth Hall which is his domain. May he help me to remember my non-phenomenal self.

Involved with manifestations of my compulsive actions,
Swirling in a hurricane of force,
Separating into primal elements,
Phenomena of consciousness.

Opening before me paths of inattention,
Nothing there but misery and pain,
Serene and calm I wait in stillness and in silence,
Bathed in cleansing radiation.

Brilliant in the light of inner vision,
I see myself so comfortably familiar,
Master of all space and time,
Manifesting all phenomena.

Penetrating radiation,
Orange explosion from his heart to mine,
Another light, soft violet, near the first,
Seems to offer refuge to my soul.

Melting in vibrating fusion,
Dissolving my resistance,
I lose the force of my reactions,
Not attracted to the violet light.

Wandering alone in worlds of habit,
Bathed in cleansing radiation,
Surrendering myself
In endless crystal waters.

All phenomena is illusion,
Neither attracted nor repelled,
Not making any sudden moves,
My habits will carry me through.

Seventh Hall

In the Seventh and last Hall is deprivation, annihilation, forgetfulness, speechlessness, soundlessness and the utter absence of sensation.

In this ocean of silent immensity, the pattern on the inner surface of the infinite polyhedron loses all its form, and the drop which can voluntarily become part of this great ocean of silence obtains for itself eternal peace.

When, eventually, I emerge from this calm eternal sea I understand the essence of Creation and the greatest of all secrets is revealed: how I can lose myself and at the same time find myself. A drop of water in the ocean is at once the wholeness of the ocean, but an ocean in a drop of water is lost in the perfection of the infinite sphere.

Forty-Third Chamber

These are the instructions for the First Chamber of the Seventh Hall of the Kingdom of Heaven.

As I experience the disintegration of my organic identity into the primal elements of consciousness in my passage through the eternal world, the tattered remnants of the world of matter surround me.

These apparitions of phenomena are my own evocations, emanating from my own primordial consciousness.

In the First Chamber of the Seventh Hall, the phantom reverberations of organic compulsions are consumed in reactions to the organic mind, evoking illusions of the phenomenal world, and my attention is caught up in this distraction.

I remember my reactions of the organic mind in my passage through the phenomenal world and, passing once again into the endless emptiness of the Void, these reactions swirl upward in my consciousness. Not swept away by them into the magnetic force of sudden rebirth, I invoke the presence of the guardian of the First Chamber of the Seventh Hall of Heaven, the angel Naamah, who is called 'she who is most pleasing', who corrupted the angels Azza and Azazel, and is known as the great seducer of spirits and of men, who in the phenomenal world was the sister of Tubal-Cain; the angel Naamah I invoke.

Brilliant violet radiation emanates from her heart, penetrating and dissolving all reverberations of the organic mind. At the same time, the phantom after-images of the phenomenal world, bathed in soft, smoky orange light, seem to offer refuge from the cleansing radiation.

Not becoming engulfed in the seductive magnetic force of rebirth, I bathe in cleansing radiation, the brilliant violet light dissolving all reverberations of the organic mind.

Wandering in the phantom images of the organic world, may my non-phenomenal self be cleansed by the brilliant radiation of the angel Naamah; may inexorable reality be my guide.

May I remain impartial to phenomena, free from organic reactions, not expelled in sudden rebirth.

May the blessed angel Naamah be my protector. May she bring me safely through the First Chamber of the Seventh Hall which is her domain. May she help me to remember my non-phenomenal self.

Involved with reactions to solid form,
Swirling in a hurricane of force,
Separating into primal elements,
Phenomena of motion.

Opening before me paths of flesh and blood,
Nothing there but misery and pain,
Serene and calm I wait in stillness and in silence,
Bathed in cleansing radiation.

Brilliant in the light of inner vision,
I see my ego struggling for breath,
Clinging tightly to the remnants of organic life,
Terrified to die.

Penetrating radiation,
Violet explosion from her heart to mine,
Another light, soft orange, near the first,
Seems to offer refuge to my soul.

Melting in vibrating fusion,
Dissolving my resistance,
I lose the force of my reactions,
Not attracted to the orange light.

Wandering alone, maintaining reactions of body symptoms,
Bathed in cleansing radiation,
Surrendering myself
In endless crystal waters.

All phenomena is illusion,
Neither attracted nor repelled,
Not making any sudden moves,
My habits will carry me through.

Forty-Fourth Chamber

These are the instructions for the Second Chamber of the Seventh Hall of the Kingdom of Heaven.

As I experience the disintegration of my organic identity into the primal elements of consciousness in my passage through the eternal world, the tattered remnants of the world of matter surround me.

These apparitions of phenomena are my own evocations, emanating from my own primordial consciousness.

In the Second Chamber of the Seventh Hall, the phantom reverberations of the organic mind are consumed in reactions to my organic identity, evoking illusions of the phenomenal world, and my attention is caught up in this distraction.

I remember my reactions of my organic identity in my passage through the phenomenal world and, passing once again into the endless emptiness of the Void, these reactions swirl upward in my consciousness. Not swept away by them into the magnetic force of sudden rebirth, I invoke the presence of the guardian of the Second Chamber of the Seventh Hall of Heaven, the angel Lilith, who was the first wife of Adam and bore him every day one-hundred children; the fiery female who first cohabited with the earliest of men, but after the creation of the second Adam and his true wife Eve, was lifted from the Earth. She who was the mother of Cain, and is the progenitor of prostitution; the angel Lilith I invoke.

Brilliant blue radiation emanates from her heart, penetrating and dissolving all reverberations of my organic identity. At the same time, the phantom after-images of the phenomenal world, bathed in soft, smoky white light, seem to offer refuge from the cleansing radiation.

Not becoming engulfed in the seductive magnetic force of rebirth, I bathe in cleansing radiation, the brilliant blue light dissolving all reverberations of the organic mind.

Wandering in the phantom images of the organic world, may my non-phenomenal self be cleansed by the brilliant radiation of the angel Lilith; may inexorable reality be my guide.

May I remain impartial to phenomena, free from organic reactions, not expelled in sudden rebirth.

May the blessed angel Lilith be my protector. May she bring me safely through the Second Chamber of the Seventh Hall which is her domain. May she help me to remember my non-phenomenal self.

Involved with reactions to my identity,
Swirling in a hurricane of force,
Separating into primal elements,
Phenomena of dimension.

Opening before me paths of time and space,
Nothing there but misery and pain,
Serene and calm I wait in stillness and in silence,
Bathed in cleansing radiation.

Brilliant in the light of inner vision,
I see myself controlling destiny,
Clinging to the content of the mind,
Frozen memory.

Penetrating radiation,
Blue explosion from her heart to mine,
Another light, soft white, near the first,
Seems to offer refuge to my soul.

Melting in vibrating fusion,
Dissolving my resistance,
I lose the force of my reactions,
Not attracted to the soft white light.

Wandering alone, maintaining reactions of ego,
Bathed in cleansing radiation,
Surrendering myself
In endless crystal waters.

All phenomena is illusion,
Neither attracted nor repelled,
Not making any sudden moves,
My habits will carry me through.

Forty-Fifth Chamber

These are the instructions for the Third Chamber of the Seventh Hall of the Kingdom of Heaven.

As I experience the disintegration of my organic identity into the primal elements of consciousness in my passage through the eternal world, the tattered remnants of the world of matter surround me.

These apparitions of phenomena are my own evocations, emanating from my own primordial consciousness.

In the Third Chamber of the Seventh Hall, the phantom reverberations of my organic identity are consumed in reactions to organic fear, evoking illusions of the phenomenal world, and my attention is caught up in this distraction.

I remember my reactions of organic fear in my passage through the phenomenal world and, passing once again into the endless emptiness of the Void, these reactions swirl upward in my consciousness. Not swept away by them into the magnetic force of sudden rebirth, I invoke the presence of the guardian of the Third Chamber of the Seventh Hall of Heaven, the angel Eisheth Zenunim, who emanated from beneath the Throne of God, and who plagues the creatures of the phenomenal world until the Judgment Day when God will make the Earth clean and take away all filth and evil from the world; the angel Eisheth Zenunim I invoke.

Brilliant white radiation emanates from her heart, penetrating and dissolving all reverberations of organic fear. At the same time, the phantom after-images of the phenomenal world, bathed in soft, smoky black light, seem to offer refuge from the cleansing radiation.

Not becoming engulfed in the seductive magnetic force of rebirth, I bathe in cleansing radiation, the brilliant white light dissolving all reverberations of the organic mind.

Wandering in the phantom images of the organic world, may my non-phenomenal self be cleansed by the brilliant radiation of the angel Eisheth Zenunim; may inexorable reality be my guide.

May I remain impartial to phenomena, free from organic reactions, not expelled in sudden rebirth.

May the blessed angel Eisheth Zenunim be my protector. May she bring me safely through the Third Chamber of the Seventh Hall which is her domain. May she help me to remember my non-phenomenal self.

Involved with reactions to anxious expectation,
Swelling upward from my hidden self,
Separating into primal form,
Illusion of phenomena.

Opening before me paths of fear and anger,
Nothing there but misery and pain,
Serene and calm I wait in stillness and in silence,
Bathed in cleansing radiation.

Brilliant in the light of inner vision,
I see myself wreathed in seething hate,
Offering no sympathy or help,
Tantalizingly superior.

Penetrating radiation,
White explosion from her heart to mine,
Another light, soft black, near the first,
Seems to offer refuge to my soul.

Melting in vibrating fusion,
Dissolving my resistance,
I lose the force of my reactions,
Not attracted to the light of smoky black.

Wandering alone in worlds of fear,
Bathed in cleansing radiation,
Surrendering myself
In endless crystal waters.

All phenomena is illusion,
Neither attracted nor repelled,
Not making any sudden moves,
My habits will carry me through.

Forty-Sixth Chamber

These are the instructions for the Fourth Chamber of the Seventh Hall of the Kingdom of Heaven.

As I experience the disintegration of my organic identity into the primal elements of consciousness in my passage through the eternal world, the tattered remnants of the world of matter surround me.

These apparitions of phenomena are my own evocations, emanating from my own primordial consciousness.

In the Fourth Chamber of the Seventh Hall, the phantom reverberations of organic fear are consumed in reactions to organic jealousy, evoking illusions of the phenomenal world, and my attention is caught up in this distraction.

I remember my reactions of organic jealousy in my passage through the phenomenal world and, passing once again into the endless emptiness of the Void, these reactions swirl upward in my consciousness. Not swept away by them into the magnetic force of sudden rebirth, I invoke the presence of the guardian of the Fourth Chamber of the Seventh Hall of Heaven, the angel Shekinah, the bride of the Invoked Presence, who redeems us from all evil, the glory emanating from God who is with those who follow and praise the Holy Law, whose work was the creation of the phenomenal world, who is called the Holy Ghost, of whom it was said, 'Behold, I send an angel before thee, to keep thee in the way', who was sent into exile with the Second Adam when he was driven from the garden, that he might labor to lead her back to God, which is the true purpose of the scriptures; the angel Shekinah I invoke.

Brilliant green radiation emanates from her heart, penetrating and dissolving all reverberations of organic jealousy. At the same time, the phantom after-images of the phenomenal world, bathed in soft, smoky red light, seem to offer refuge from the cleansing radiation.

Not becoming engulfed in the seductive magnetic force of rebirth, I bathe in cleansing radiation, the brilliant green light dissolving all reverberations of the organic mind.

Wandering in the phantom images of the organic world, may my non-phenomenal self be cleansed by the brilliant radiation of the angel Shekinah; may inexorable reality be my guide.

May I remain impartial to phenomena, free from organic reactions, not expelled in sudden rebirth.

May the blessed angel Shekinah be my protector. May she bring me safely through the Fourth Chamber of the Seventh Hall which is her domain. May she help me to remember my non-phenomenal self.

Involved with reactions to jealousy and competition,
Rising upward from my hidden self,
Separating into primal form,
Repulsively attractive.

Opening before me paths of lingering uncertainty,
Nothing there but misery and pain,
Serene and calm I wait in stillness and in silence,
Bathed in cleansing radiation.

Brilliant in the light of inner vision,
I see myself suspiciously distrustful,
Clinging to my every action,
Gnawing at my soul.

Penetrating radiation,
Green explosion from her heart to mine,
Another light, soft red, near the first,
Seems to offer refuge to my soul.

Melting in vibrating fusion,
Dissolving my resistance,
I lose the force of my reactions,
Not attracted to the soft red light.

Wandering alone in worlds of jealousy,
Bathed in cleansing radiation,
Surrendering myself
In endless crystal waters.

All phenomena is illusion,
Neither attracted nor repelled,
Not making any sudden moves,
My habits will carry me through.

Forty-Seventh Chamber

These are the instructions for the Fifth Chamber of the Seventh Hall of the Kingdom of Heaven.

As I experience the disintegration of my organic identity into the primal elements of consciousness in my passage through the eternal world, the tattered remnants of the world of matter surround me.

These apparitions of phenomena are my own evocations, emanating from my own primordial consciousness.

In the Fifth Chamber of the Seventh Hall, the phantom reverberations of organic jealousy are consumed in reactions to organic self-pity, evoking illusions of the phenomenal world, and my attention is caught up in this distraction.

I remember my reactions of organic self-pity in my passage through the phenomenal world and, passing once again into the endless emptiness of the Void, these reactions swirl upward in my consciousness. Not swept away by them into the magnetic force of sudden rebirth, I invoke the presence of the guardian of the Fifth Chamber of the Seventh Hall of Heaven, the angel Pistis Sophia, who is called 'the faith of wisdom', a great *Aeon*, who created for God the superior angels in the Citadel of Heaven; the angel Pistis Sophia I invoke.

Brilliant yellow radiation emanates from her heart, penetrating and dissolving all reverberations of organic self-pity. At the same time, the phantom after-images of the phenomenal world, bathed in soft, smoky blue light, seem to offer refuge from the cleansing radiation.

Not becoming engulfed in the seductive magnetic force of rebirth, I bathe in cleansing radiation, the brilliant yellow light dissolving all reverberations of the organic mind.

Wandering in the phantom images of the organic world, may my non-phenomenal self be cleansed by the brilliant radiation of the angel Pistis Sophia; may inexorable reality be my guide.

May I remain impartial to phenomena, free from organic reactions, not expelled in sudden rebirth.

May the blessed angel Pistis Sophia be my protector. May she bring me safely through the Fifth Chamber of the Seventh Hall which is her domain. May she help me to remember my non-phenomenal self.

Involved with reactions to vanity and arrogance,
Towering above myself in pride,
Separating into primal form,
Immovably secure.

Opening before me paths of isolation,
Nothing there but misery and pain,
Serene and calm I wait in stillness and in silence,
Bathed in cleansing radiation.

Brilliant in the light of inner vision,
I see myself inferior and foolish,
Holding tightly to the past and present,
Terrified to bend.

Penetrating radiation,
Yellow explosion from her heart to mine,
Another light, soft blue, near the first,
Seems to offer refuge to my soul.

Melting in vibrating fusion,
Dissolving my resistance,
I lose the force of my reactions,
Not attracted to the soft blue light.

Wandering alone in worlds of pride,
Bathed in cleansing radiation,
Surrendering myself
In endless crystal waters.

All phenomena is illusion,
Neither attracted nor repelled,
Not making any sudden moves,
My habits will carry me through.

Forty-Eighth Chamber

These are the instructions for the Sixth Chamber of the Seventh Hall of the Kingdom of Heaven.

As I experience the disintegration of my organic identity into the primal elements of consciousness in my passage through the eternal world, the tattered remnants of the world of matter surround me.

These apparitions of phenomena are my own evocations, emanating from my own primordial consciousness.

In the Sixth Chamber of the Seventh Hall, the phantom reverberations of organic self-pity are consumed in reactions to organic hunger, evoking illusions of the phenomenal world, and my attention is caught up in this distraction.

I remember my reactions of organic hunger in my passage through the phenomenal world and, passing once again into the endless emptiness of the Void, these reactions swirl upward in my consciousness. Not swept away by them into the magnetic force of sudden rebirth, I invoke the presence of the guardian of the Sixth Chamber of the Seventh Hall of Heaven, the angel Barbelo, who is a great *Archon*, next in rank to Our Endless Creator, who was called upon by God to assist in the creation of all angels in the Heavens; the angel Barbelo I invoke.

Brilliant red radiation emanates from her heart, penetrating and dissolving all reverberations of organic hunger. At the same time, the phantom after-images of the phenomenal world, bathed in soft, smoky yellow light, seem to offer refuge from the cleansing radiation.

Not becoming engulfed in the seductive magnetic force of rebirth, I bathe in cleansing radiation, the brilliant red light dissolving all reverberations of the organic mind.

Wandering in the phantom images of the organic world, may my non-phenomenal self be cleansed by the brilliant radiation of the angel Barbelo; may inexorable reality be my guide.

May I remain impartial to phenomena, free from organic reactions, not expelled in sudden rebirth.

May the blessed angel Barbelo be my protector. May she bring me safely through the Sixth Chamber of the Seventh Hall which is her domain. May she help me to remember my non-phenomenal self.

Thirty-Ninth Chamber

These are the instructions for the Fourth Chamber of the Sixth Hall of the Kingdom of Heaven.

As I experience the disintegration of my organic identity into the primal elements of consciousness in my passage through the eternal world, the tattered remnants of the world of matter surround me.

These apparitions of phenomena are my own evocations, emanating from my own primordial consciousness.

In the Fourth Chamber of the Sixth Hall, the phantom reverberations of organic fear are consumed in manifestations of organic jealousy, evoking illusions of the phenomenal world, and my attention is caught up in this distraction.

I remember the manifestations of organic jealousy in my passage through the phenomenal world and, passing once again into the endless emptiness of the Void, these manifestations swirl upward in my consciousness. Not swept away by them into the magnetic force of sudden rebirth, I invoke the presence of the guardian of the Fourth Chamber of the Sixth Hall of Heaven, the angel Abel, who judges souls which arrive in Heaven; who is one of twelve of the Order of Powers which issued from the angel Ialdabaoth, who rules on the Lord's Day, before whom every soul must appear for weighing and judgment, to be recorded by Enoch in the Book of Records; the angel Abel I invoke.

Brilliant green radiation emanates from his heart, penetrating and dissolving all reverberations of organic jealousy. At the same time, the phantom after-images of the phenomenal world, bathed in soft, smoky red light, seem to offer refuge from the cleansing radiation.

Not becoming engulfed in the seductive magnetic force of rebirth, I bathe in cleansing radiation, the brilliant green light dissolving all reverberations of the organic mind.

Wandering in the phantom images of the organic world, may my non-phenomenal self be cleansed by the brilliant radiation of the angel Abel; may inexorable reality be my guide.

May I remain impartial to phenomena, free from organic manifestations, not expelled in sudden rebirth.

May the blessed angel Abel be my protector. May he bring me safely through the Fourth Chamber of the Sixth Hall which is his domain. May he help me to remember my non-phenomenal self.

Involved with reactions to passionate possession,
Liberated from illusion of phenomena,
Separating into primal form,
Phenomena of senses.

Opening before me paths of endless passion,
Nothing there but misery and pain,
Serene and calm I wait in stillness and in silence,
Bathed in cleansing radiation.

Brilliant in the light of inner vision,
I see myself seductive and compelling,
Searching endlessly for satisfaction,
Always wanting more.

Penetrating radiation,
Red explosion from her heart to mine,
Another light, soft yellow, near the first,
Seems to offer refuge to my soul.

Melting in vibrating fusion,
Dissolving my resistance,
I lose the force of my reactions,
Not attracted to the yellow light.

Wandering alone among the hungry souls,
Bathed in cleansing radiation,
Surrendering myself
In endless crystal waters.

All phenomena is illusion,
Neither attracted nor repelled,
Not making any sudden moves,
My habits will carry me through.

Forty-Ninth Chamber

These are the instructions for the Seventh Chamber of the Seventh Hall of the Kingdom of Heaven.

As I experience the disintegration of my organic identity into the primal elements of consciousness in my passage through the eternal world, the tattered remnants of the world of matter surround me.

These apparitions of phenomena are my own evocations, emanating from my own primordial consciousness.

In the Seventh Chamber of the Seventh Hall, the phantom reverberations of organic hunger are consumed in reactions to organic compulsions, evoking illusions of the phenomenal world, and my attention is caught up in this distraction.

I remember my reactions of organic compulsions in my passage through the phenomenal world and, passing once again into the endless emptiness of the Void, these reactions swirl upward in my consciousness. Not swept away by them into the magnetic force of sudden rebirth, I invoke the presence of the guardian of the Seventh Chamber of the Seventh Hall of Heaven, the angel Ashtoreth, who seduces those of the world of spirit to descend to the phenomenal world, and who is the daughter of Lilith and mother of all mortal men; the angel Ashtoreth I invoke.

Brilliant orange radiation emanates from her heart, penetrating and dissolving all reverberations of organic compulsions. At the same time, the phantom after-images of the phenomenal world, bathed in soft, smoky violet light, seem to offer refuge from the cleansing radiation.

Not becoming engulfed in the seductive magnetic force of rebirth, I bathe in cleansing radiation, the brilliant orange light dissolving all reverberations of the organic mind.

Wandering in the phantom images of the organic world, may my non-phenomenal self be cleansed by the brilliant radiation of the angel Ashtoreth; may inexorable reality be my guide.

May I remain impartial to phenomena, free from organic reactions, not expelled in sudden rebirth.

May the blessed angel Ashtoreth be my protector. May she bring me safely through the Seventh Chamber of the Seventh Hall which is her domain. May she help me to remember my non-phenomenal self.

Involved with reactions to my compulsive actions,
Swirling in a hurricane of force,
Separating into primal elements,
Phenomena of consciousness.

Opening before me paths of inattention,
Nothing there but misery and pain,
Serene and calm I wait in stillness and in silence,
Bathed in cleansing radiation.

Brilliant in the light of inner vision,
I see myself so comfortably familiar,
Master of all space and time,
Manifesting all phenomena.

Penetrating radiation,
Orange explosion from her heart to mine,
Another light, soft violet, near the first,
Seems to offer refuge to my soul.

Melting in vibrating fusion,
Dissolving my resistance,
I lose the force of my reactions,
Not attracted to the violet light.

Wandering alone in worlds of habit,
Bathed in cleansing radiation,
Surrendering myself
In endless crystal waters.

All phenomena is illusion,
Neither attracted nor repelled,
Not making any sudden moves,
My habits will carry me through.

THIRD STAGE

Recognition Factors

A feeling of supernormal perception, visions of events happening far off in time and space; supernormal powers far beyond the ordinary limits of organic laws.

I am being operated like a puppet on a stage; hollow sounds of mocking laughter. Apprehension. An impending earthquake, flood, storm, tidal wave, nuclear explosion; the urge to get out no matter what; no reasonable explanation for this apprehension.

A compulsive urge to wander restlessly, driven by a silent, powerful, inexorable wind; brief moments of rest and relaxation at all the familiar places.

Cold, clammy deadness; isolated from surrounding life, emerging from deep sleep, a sudden jolt awake. Anxiety about the body; various phenomenal forms vanish unexpectedly, provoking ironic laughter.

Selecting Rebirth

In the mirror,
Visions mask the emptiness.
Ancient faces,
Many younger ones.

Selecting pathways through phenomena,
Guard against the force of apprehension;
A long and happy life may be unprofitable
For evolution of the soul.

Opening the eyes to other options,
Waiting patiently for understanding,
Choosing paths which feed the spirit,
Among the faces of the dead.

Struggle disappears,
Symptoms vanish.
Flowing, ever-changing
Ancient-new Creation.
No need for explanation
When blending with the flow.

Gush into the ocean of life;
Float in the Sea of Phenomena.
No need for talk or action.
Inexorable return.

Descending Angels in the darkness;
Erotic worship in the Light;
Illusion of phenomena.

Close to Liberation;
Whatever I think I see, the King is naked.
Things will never be the same.
Was this all a dream?

The image melts away;
Dreams and apparitions echoing the past;
Unborn, unceasing self;
Water flowing into water.

Impartially returning to the organic vision,
Without attraction or repulsion;
A gentle passage from one world to another;
Voluntary rebirth.

Glossary

Body of Habits
The non-phenomenal phantom body similar in its habits, perceptions and reactions to the organic body, which remains with the Voyager throughout Transit.

Chamber
One of forty-nine distinct spaces in the Second Stage of Transit, each ruled over by a particular Angelic Entity who is the guardian of that Chamber.

Cleansing Radiation
Seven colored lights of the non-phenomenal world that burn away those tendencies and involvements which cause the Voyager to be ejected from the non-phenomenal world into the lower worlds of rebirth.

Clear Light
A clear, colorless light in endless extension. The basic substance of the non-phenomenal world.

Conscious
Able to tolerate ever-flowing change, to accept all formations as they appear, and to know that all phenomena is illusion, within which is the real, non-phenomenal, world.

Ego
The manifestation of a crystallized and conditioned phenomenal consciousness.

Expulsion
The moment of separation and expansion, either voluntary or involuntary, from the phenomenal world into the non-phenomenal world.

Incarnation
The attention of the source-of-personal-attention rooted, usually involuntarily, in the perceptions and sensations of the world of phenomena.

Hall
One of seven passageways through the Second Stage of Transit, each of which shows a unique vision of the non-phenomenal world.

Hallucination
Phenomenal afterimages perpetuated by momentum of organic habits, projected on the non-phenomenal.

Karma
Habits of the organic world which guarantee that tomorrow will be basically the same as today.

Non-phenomenal
Of, or relating to, the non-differentiated world outside space, time and separate objects.

Non-phenomenal lifestyle
A lifestyle within the organic phenomenal world, which corresponds to a lifestyle of the non-phenomenal world, to avoid

Expulsion into sudden rebirth, or 'coming down'.

Phenomenal
Of, or relating to, the fragmented hallucination of separate objects, space and time.

Radiation
A non-reflected source of light; self-luminosity.

Rebirth
Re-entry into an organic lifeform; the formation of a new subjective phenomenal blanket over the eternal, non-phenomenal world.

Reader
An individual who takes on the responsibility to deliver the readings from the *New American Book of the Dead* in order to guide the Voyager through the Transit state or for healing.

Resonance
The phenomenon of sympathetic vibration occurring between the Reader and the Voyager when contact has been established.

Transit
The between-lives state; the state of existence in the non-phenomenal world between excursions into the phenomenal world.

Transition
The period during the passage from phenomenal perceptions to non-phenomenal perceptions.

Vigil
The series of readings which take place in the hour following Expulsion from the organic form.

Voyager
The spiritual part of the human being that goes into Transit after separation from the organic body.

Index

Dear Reader of the *New American Book of the Dead:*

Having completed this book, you may feel the wish to be of service to all Beings everywhere by applying the Teaching contained in the *New American Book of the Dead.* If you wish to pursue this path further, a professional Transit Practitioner's Course is offered by correspondence and, in certain areas of the country, through study groups.

The Transit Practitioner's Course teaches you to be competent in dealing with those who are dying, to prepare them for Expulsion, and to maintain a close, strong contact with them throughout the complete Transit cycle of 53 days. A privately published Practitioner's edition of the *New American Book of the Dead* is also available, as well as an Advanced Transit Practitioner's Training Manual for those who have already developed the beginning skills of a Transit Practitioner.

For more information about the Transit Practitioner's Course or either of the related publications, please write to:

I.D.H.H.B., Inc.
P.O. Box 370, Department A
Nevada City, CA. 95959